# ESCAPING THE KNIGHT IN DIRTY BLUE JEANS

## Laney Wind

ISBN-13:
978-1717437525
ISBN-10:
1717437524

Cover picture by Wina Rushing.
Edits by Devin Brown.

Although "Escaping the Knight in Dirty Blue Jeans" is a contemporary memoir, all characters, organizations, places and events have been changed to protect the innocent.

References to Bible verses are from the following translations: New King James Version ©1982 Thomas Nelson Publishers, King James Version ©1611 Oxford Church of England, and the New Living Translation ©2005 Tyndale House Publishers.

Printed in the United States of America

*Dedicated to:*

I dedicate this book to the first woman I ever faced my fears with. I spoke and she believed me.

My dearest Aunt Bev, you showed me I could trust someone.

So many ways you have impacted my life: aunt, spiritual mother, best friend, confidant, mentor, prayer partner, writing buddy, art lovers.

I cannot bear to think where my girls and I would be without you.

Thank you for being who you are and loving me for who I am.

You know me better than anyone on this earth beside the Lord himself. I am so blessed to get to laugh, cry, be silent, sob, act silly, mess up, be expressive and talk about His Goodness with you.

How very precious and loved you are!

## MY KNIGHT OR MY CAPTOR?

"Why did you stay?" the officer asked.

A blank stare. *Was this a question they were supposed to ask me?* "That's hard to explain."

I struggled to give him rational answers to an irrational question, "Maybe I held onto hope of him getting better…?"

Would this answer make sense to a police officer?

Are they going to take Jacob away? Did I act too fast? Not wait long enough for my husband to leave sufficient evidence? I finally called. I moved. But did I do it too soon? My bruises have almost faded away, so will they arrest him? If he comes back tonight, I do not know what will happen.

My heart raced. Could they hear it? I swear it was thumping out of my eardrums.

I could not stop my fumbling fingers as my hands shook. It physically hurt as I showed the officer photos on my phone. My bruises. Too many pictures. My portfolio of pain.

*Breathe. Please, Laney, breathe. You can do this.* I am going to pass out, freak out, panic, cry, beg and scream. PLEASE take him. I have to hold it together. *Be strong. Just be strong.*

↓↓↓

In the beginning, I called him "My knight in dirty blue jeans." We met at work in an automotive plant working on chasses. He was a welder, so "dirty blue jeans."

The "knight" turned out to be quite the cliché. Not at first, of course. Back then, I was not into *red flags*. I had spiraled down a dark hole that tried to swallow me.

Yet there he was. Jacob. A pretense of strength, stability and just enough steadiness to pull me out. But that was all a deception. An illusion.

The rose-colored glasses I wore already thickened by years of broken promises and misplaced trust. With my own set of problems, hurts and needs that could no longer be numbed in all the usual self-destructive ways, I burned inside. Scorched by pain.

So I was too blind to see or too close to the bottom of that pit to care. I needed a glimpse, a sparkle of something. Something strong and solid to hold on to.

He saw my need. And THAT seeing was what he needed.

At first it was kind of sweet. Cute even. We both worked third shift, so he would come over after work every day. Emotionally messed up from a two-year relationship that ended badly, plus the recent death of a prior boyfriend, I was not looking for another relationship. Not seriously—on the outside.

So tired. So hurt. When I discussed Jacob with my friend she responded, "Big deal. Just have some fun. It's not like you're going to marry the guy."

So much for that game plan.

He seemed to want to be around my family, do what I wanted to do and look out for my interests. But he changed into a controller. I just did not recognize it.

Jacob's demands, I viewed as strengths—a man who knew what he wanted. I had done what I wanted for so long in my life, felt as if no one cared enough to confront me, I was drawn to him. My intentions were to still do what I wanted, with whom I wanted. But I never found the opportunity. When we were not at work, he never left me alone.

Little things he told me did not seem to add up right. But at the time they seemed trivial. I did not know how involved I had become. I was having fun, enjoying the attention, the caring, the time together. Who really cared about the crazy stories or little lies he told? I dismissed them.

Stuffed them down with all the other mess I stuffed away. The same lies I brushed – off were lies I believed over eighteen years. Except they could not hide anymore.

The problem with lies is you can never really trust someone you cannot believe.

When the next lie comes or an old one resurfaces, that trust factor goes right out the window.

It cannot rebuild because it was never built.

I grasped onto something I hoped was true. Even if it was not truth at least maybe something about it, something about the "us" part could BE true.

How could we build a relationship on lies, distrust, and emotional problems?

Lies could start for many reasons: shame, guilt, embarrassment, to impress. They could even be used to cover those we loved. Lies happened for all the wrong reasons and all the right excuses—that is what we told ourselves. I was not without fault of my own. I understood the trap and felt empathy.

When I was a child, my mother would say, "Oh, what a wicked web we weave, when at first we practice to deceive." I thought she was senile. Now I know she was wise.

One small lie leads to the next, which leads to the bigger one, until they have all intertwined. To cover the first little "tale" another one of a slightly bigger size has to follow and another ear catching story must happen.

The deceiver simply cannot stop. This huge web of lies is woven. You are either the spider and keep "spinning" those venomous lies or realize you are a fly caught in the web. Stuck. Fearful. Unable to get away from all the deceit.

My whole life I had heard a man could feel trapped into staying with a woman. I knew now it worked both ways.

I felt trapped. I was that fly in Jacob's web of lies.

Besides, he was always sorry and it was not too bad—at first.

## WHITE FLAG / RED FLAGS

Bloody noses.  Broken bones.  Blackened eyes.

"You have to add more detail." As these words come out of my aunt's mouth, I pause, stop reading and look up at her. We are close. I know enough to pay attention.

With wisdom, she reminds me I need details of the abuse. Without details I might not be clear enough. Exactly what does violence and abuse look like without the broken bones, busted noses or horrible black eyes?

So I painstakingly bend over to pick up the boulders instead of toss tiny pebbles. With rebuilt muscles in place of atrophied arms, I lift the rocks and hurl what weighs heavy and hard.

I speak the truth. Truth is the only thing that tears down the web of lies and sets us free.

Early in our relationship Jacob shared with me how he had been victimized as a child. Did I believe him? I had shared with him that I was. I had more than my share of childhood trauma. But I had to believe his truth. For a person to be able to do, say and be who he was, he too must have suffered greatly.

Though his past does not excuse his actions.

But to have some kind of solace, to be able to make the tiniest bit of sense of any of the madness: I HAD to believe Jacob was also someone's victim—before we became his.

In February of 1995, we sort of started dating. I convinced myself it was only about having some fun. So I agreed to his terms of seeing him exclusively but planned to continue to do exactly what I wanted. Something I viewed at the time as strength became a red flag—a form of control.

Could I not see how far out in the ocean I swam? How deep in the water I was? So close to drowning.

So tired, I hurt. My heart ached. I was tired of life.

I never blamed God. I may have wondered why about something here or there. But blame God or get truly angry with him? I cannot remember ever doing so. I knew he never quite left me.

Taking full accountability of things that happened or did not happen was never an issue. I wore guilt well. It fit like an anchor chained to my soul.

I drifted. Not aware how deep I was. The waves crashed on top of me as they tried to take me under. Alcohol and drugs no longer worked to numb the wretched pain and weariness. *God? Do you hear me? Do you see me?*

The "white" flag of surrender was close to being held up in my hand.

But God was a restorer not a destroyer of hearts, of relationships. He always gave us a choice. God could turn things around for good.

Was Jacob an answer to my prayers? Or the tsunami I never saw coming?

✝✝✝

By November of that same year, I was pregnant. A few years before, my ten year-old daughter and I had moved back in with my parents. One night, she and my parents were out of town. Jacob came over and he was angry.

He was ballistic about the pregnancy. Livid because I would not agree to an abortion. Like a raging beast, he paced up and down the long hallway. Past my smiling family photos that lined the dark paneled walls.

I pleaded, "Please calm down. Why are you acting like this?"

My body quivered from the struggle to contain his screams.

"I'll take care of it then."

He grabbed the kitchen broom and stormed toward me. "I'll shove this broom up you."

The panic. My heart raced. *What do I do? Oh my God, what do I do?*

He towered over me, broom in hand, as I tried to reason with him. This crazed, wild animal look in his eyes. Anger permeated through his skin—the smell of sweat filled my nostrils.

*Don't let him see how afraid you are. Act strong. Protect the baby. Fight back.* So scared. JESUS, I was scared.

In desperation, I ran to the phone and pushed random buttons. *I don't know his grandmothers number. Let this work. Please, God.*

"You're out of control. I'm calling your grandmother." I sobbed.

The melt down began. After what felt like an eternity, Jacob's rage started to calm. He pleaded. He apologized. Then the excuses for why he did what he did: he never had a child before, how would he support it? Where would we live? He would not be a good father.

"But…Laney, this will NEVER happen again."

Jacob wept. I wept.

Is this shock? What just happened? I could tell no one. Not my family. I promised myself I would never get pregnant again unless I was married. Responsibilities that came with a child were huge. My mother had helped me raise my wonderful daughter.

Now, 10 years later, I had messed up and was trapped. Another precious baby, and I was trapped. He said he was sorry. "Everything will be okay," he promised.

And it was…for a while.

↓↓↓

"I now pronounce you husband and wife. Jacob, you may kiss the bride."

Uncontrollable tears stained my face as he bent down to seal the commitment. On a cold, winter night of 1996, my father, an ordained pastor, married us in my parent's family room.

Surrounded by a TV, plaid living room suite and wearing my mother's veil she took her vows in, it was a far cry from a church wedding. The blue jeans that accompanied the sacred cream colored lace veil had to do. At least I had some of my family there to witness, it could have been worse.

Was this overwhelming emotion hope? Hope that I might have a family—a father for my children and a husband who loved me? Hope that life would work out and everything might be okay? Did I weep with hope?

For a moment my thoughts drifted....

"Why get married?" my friend Maxwell asked, "Y'all are already living together. Wait at least another year or so."

One of the few times I was ever alone, Maxwell took advantage to give his opinion.

"Because he loves me, I love him, to give Millie a name, so she has a father...." Sound, sensible reasons, right?

Maxwell stared at me and shook his head. He was not swayed. "You have lost your mind."

*Things will get better. Everyone fights. Heck. Maxwell and Macey have a good fight every now and then and they are just fine. Look at my mom and dad. I had seen how he mistreated my mom all my life. I had watched this angry man.*

*Grew up with his harmful behavior toward my siblings and me. All of us unaware we held up our right hands and took a silent oath to protect the secrets. Don't talk about it. Pretend it's normal and live that way. We grew up in it, survived, until it became our normal.*

*Maybe I thought Jacob, this man I married, would be different. He would get better. It would get better. My hope for my normal. Why shouldn't this marriage work?*

And I kissed my husband back.

Perfect. Oh, how my heart melted for my second child.

A few months prior to the wedding, on September 22, our daughter was born. A beautiful baby. She neither looked more like him nor me but was intricately created to resemble both.

Two daughters. Two lives I was responsible for while I paddled to keep afloat.

Before Millie was born, Jacob and I found a place to live. Our life seemed okay during the "honeymoon" period.

This fantasy life built within my castle walls did not last long.

When I went on maternity leave, finances had been hit hard. With the added pressure of a baby, in crept "episodes." So unaware of how stress triggered episodes, I missed more red flags.

Jacob was angry again. What was the cause? What was the trigger? Was Millie asleep? Try as I could I could not remember. Did it really matter? He was angry. We were fighting.

*Why do I still have to be so independent? Why couldn't I just back down?*

Not wanting to show him weakness and fear as he screamed and ranted about why he felt what he felt. I would not back down.

"Stop acting like an idiot!" and "What's wrong with you?" I yelled back.

I was the matador who waved the red flag in front of the tormented bull, waiting to charge. Not smart.

The door slammed on his way out. The walls groaned. I stood in the middle of the family room of our two-bedroom trailer. Utterly distraught. Silence.

Dazed, blurred eyes scanned around for the glasses my husband slapped off my face. How was I ever going to find them? My body trembled.

Finally, thank God. Unbroken, they lay near the hallway. Relieved to see again, I took inventory of the small room.

I was horrified.

The coffee table had been flipped over in his last ditch effort to vent more aggression on his way out the door. Dark, black soil with tiny white beads fanned across the carpet where he knocked over the potted plant. Which was louder: the silence or the screaming in my head?

Comatose, I stood there.

My face stung from the fresh smack and tears trickled down my hot cheek. *What had I done? What had I gotten myself and my girls into?*

I did the only thing I knew to do. I bent over and started cleaning up Jacob's rage.

## ISOLATION TO DESOLATION

Numbly, I began to make his mess look neat. So when he came home and he was sorry—because he always was—everything would be normal again.

Pretty. Not chaotic. At least on the outside.

On the inside, it was not so beautiful, not so clean. On the inside, shadows had formed and walls closed in. How had I become so isolated?

Did it start with the decision for me to stay home with Millie? Because we both worked third shift, things were complicated. I had friends at my job. Or so I thought. A few of us kept in contact—for a while.

This arrangement seemed okay with him although it alienated me. Would it have worked better with a husband who was not so quick to anger? A man who liked some of my friends? What if I had better understood his moods?

"If it wasn't for all your bills we might have some money." Jacob pounded these words into my head. "It would be so much easier," he spewed.

Was it really all my fault? What if I had not brought debt into our marriage? Would he handle things better? Not get down so much? Or get so mad?

Sometimes my mother and I talked about money problems. She helped however she could. But I never discussed with her my secrets. Finances, yes. But nothing else.

Mother married Dad. I married Jacob. Family secrets.

Sh-h-h.

↓↓↓

Over time, I lost touch with my friends. Not many phone calls for social gatherings. My excuses seemed to work well for the behaviors happening in this life I lived. I had a baby now. More responsibility. Not as easy to find a sitter for two kids. Less time to party and hang out. So understandable, I told myself.

These reasons to try and feel better no longer worked. I felt so isolated—so alone—disconnected from everyone. Yet not connected to Jacob.

*Why did I have such awful feelings? Shouldn't I be able to talk to the man I married? Share things with him? Yet, I couldn't. A few times, I tried. Somehow it became about him. So twisted. Why did I try? Did I have moments of false security and think he might listen? Or was it just a time of distress?*

I put on a lot of weight—another side effect of my loneliness and isolation. Now another culprit to add to the list of reasons for weight gain. My weight and I had played the "now you see me, now you don't" game over the years. It was back for a visit. More shame for me.

Jacob did not mind the lack of a social life. His buddy hung around for a few years. They played cards or watched a movie. This seemed to satisfy him.

It never seemed to bother him that I had no one but him.

The rare times we went to a party or a get-together, there never failed to be a drill session after. Someone had looked at him weird or not at all.

"Did you hear how Maxwell talked to me?" "Did you see how Sammy ignored me?" and "Why did you say that?" or "Why did you look that way…? He glared at me as he waited for my response.

Nothing I countered with made sense to him. Why did he always have issues? I could not understand.

Found myself on edge around people, so I learned to watch their behaviors. See if I saw what Jacob would accuse me of later. Be prepared to support him or try to clarify the situation.

When we saw my family at holidays or special occasions, the same obsessions happened. It wore on me. His fixations almost always grew into an argument.

"Why do you always take up for everyone else?" He bellowed. "You never understand me. Why won't you listen to me?" He questioned me for hours.

"How can you not understand I am trying to help you see things differently?" I asked in exhaustion. "Everyone is not out to make you feel stupid, to give you nasty looks or say some smart-mouthed thing to you."

He was angry and unfazed.

It was a losing battle. A battle this princess should not have to fight. If he was my knight, then I was his princess. Right? But I was losing—ready to lay down the sword I should have never needed. My hope dwindled. I was ready to surrender—once again.

My isolation helped keep me silent. If I could not tell anyone before, I surely could not now. Over the years, the physical, emotional and mental stresses wore me down till I reached the point of hopelessness. Our situation would never change. Would I eventually lose my mind?

Still, I was not at my deepest darkest hour. But I was on my way.

What about the beginning of us? Back to the sweet things I could not forget.

The things that seemed normal but were meant to draw me in. If I would have seen how they intertwined with lies, abuse and deceit—all the red flags—could I have saved us?

It started with a card for an occasion or at other times simply because he wanted to. A stuffed kitty when I had a bad doctor visit. Beautiful flowers for a surprise. These simple "wooing" strategies worked wonders on someone in the place of loneliness and desperation. Why could I not see the trap?

A glittered card soon became an apology note turned ugly. It was connected to hurt and pain, not romance and love. Was our life ever about love? Or was it only about control? Then the cards, the flowers, the other sweet things stopped coming at all.

On my knees, surrounded by cartons of pink and red variegated impatiens, hands clothed in garden gloves— I sobbed. I cried like I had not cried in months. Maybe years. In the middle of the flowers I had splurged and bought, I reached a point of total desperation, isolation, loneliness and shame. The overwhelming emotions never before felt at such a deep level. Most of my life I had tried to stay too numb to feel anything.

I began to pray. As a young girl I had been baptized. But I was not an innocent child anymore. How was I worthy to plead to Jesus now? Was I too far gone? I had to try. Did anyone see me or hear me? I prayed outside beside our trailer. Did not care who heard me. Jacob was at work and I was free to weep. My heart ached.

I was blind and scared. How could we keep going financially, emotionally, or any way? I cried out to God.

Other than an occasional crisis prayer, it had been such a long time since I called out to Jesus. "I don't know what to do, God." I screamed. "What should I do?" I pleaded, tears flooding down my cheeks.

After I had exhausted myself, I sat there among the dirt. My body worn. My tear-stained face.

"Do you even hear me, Jesus?" I whispered with trembling lips.

In the silence, I heard, "Go to church."

Breathless and stunned, "Okay, Jesus. Okay, Father," I repeated without hesitation.

There was very little certainty in my life, but one thing I knew that second.

I had heard the voice of God.

## ALMOST GONE

"Will you come down with me?" Our eyes met as I whispered my request.

My baby sister nodded.

Knuckles white as death as if all the life had been drained out of them, I gripped the chair in front of me. So tight, resisting the pull in my body drawn to the preacher. Scared to take that step—the open surrender and rededication to Jesus Christ that could change my life in ways I was not ready for. Ways I could not begin to understand.

Yet, I was ready. It had been over two years since God told me to go to church. *Now here you are. Knowing you should be down at that altar, Laney. You pry those fingers off that chair and move before it's too late.*

My hands slid off the cold, metal chair. Arms fell to my sides. No more fighting.

When I stepped out into the aisle, Beth followed. The sweet support I needed to get my feet to budge. Nothing and no one could have stopped me. With a heart that raced, this time not from fear—hope maybe?—my body flew as if it could not get there fast enough.

"When I cried out to you those years before, you heard me. You patiently waited for me to take these steps." I whispered to my Jesus. "You never left me. Then, you undeniably tugged at my heart."

From that moment on, my heart belonged to God.

"In the day when I cried out, You answered me, and made me bold with strength in my soul" (Psalm 138:3 NKJV).

"Give me strength, Lord."

Overwhelmed with emotions on the drive home, questions rose. Should I share with Jacob what happened at church? How would he respond or would he respond at all? Would he be happy for me? Or would he laugh?

One thing was sure—I was different.

Haunted by the knowledge my circumstances were not different, confusion gripped me. Would I tell him? Excitement at my salvation, hope for change and a church I liked. The other part of me consumed with whatever mood he would be in once I reached the house.

The crunch of eggs shells in my ears, those we walk on around Jacob. The weight of heaviness on my shoulders, sadness and pretense.

This time I did not drive home alone. Jesus went with me. A flicker of hope after all.

†††

By the time Amelia was sixteen and Millie was four, we were in church more often. Things seemed good at home as long as no real life issues entered our lives. I tried to keep the road smooth. That was my job. But when life happened, it really happened. Life determined whether we went to church or not, the atmosphere on the thirty minute drive to church and if I could worship when I arrived.

Our car could be filled with sounds of girlie giggles and family talk. Or a ride of silence while only Jacob reined. The smell of coffee reminded me to drink it. Swallow that sweetness along with the bitter words that tried to lash out at him, *"Can't we go to church in peace?"* Sometimes Jacob did not care if we were almost at church and he was still screaming, spit flying out of his mouth.

*Get out and act pretty. Get it together quick, Laney. No tears. Jacob doesn't like our tears. People can't see them either. No tears.*

Church was another place to cover everything.

Church should have been a place that set us free. Not somewhere we still had to hide. Why was I hiding?

When we did show up, I acted as if he had not kept me up half the night, drilling me over and over with the same questions. As if he never cornered me, squeezed my face or any of the other things he chose to do. I looked the role for church. Hid any bruises. The happy, blessed couple.

I had no choice. I had to hear the pastor, to be in the atmosphere of people who had the same desire for God. But I could not tell my secrets. To protect my family was my duty.

God was changing me. I quit drinking, smoking and no more drugs. God could also change Jacob. Sometimes we made it to church without arguments. Weeks even. Divorce was not an option.

I *longed* for church. My safe haven even though I hid my secrets. Less isolated, little by little. The wall of desolation had begun to crack. Little peeks of light shone through.

✝✝✝

One night, I started to drift off when God whispered, "Deuteronomy 6:18." Amazed, I turned on the lamp and grabbed my Bible.

"What are you doing?" Jacob slurred.

"Sorry. God gave me a verse and I have to look it up."

"Well, hurry up and get the light off," he mumbled, not as impressed as me.

I was good with that. Excited to see what the scripture was. If Jacob went back to sleep without a fuss, that was perfect.

*"And thou shalt do that which is right and good in the sight of the Lord: that it will be well with thee, and that thou mayest go in and possess the good land which the Lord swore unto thy fathers."*

Touched with astonishment and joy, I cried in silence. "Show me what is right, Lord. Show me what is good," fell off my damp lips as I turned off the lamp and tried to sleep.

No doubts. Once again, I heard the voice of God.

↓↓↓

When I signed up to volunteer in the children's ministry, I felt connected to something—to people. It felt as if I was doing something right. Something good.

Loving on those babies was something I was good at, and I was faithful to show up. When those papers were signed, I committed. Like the commitment spoken of in my marriage vows.

When I went to church, my Millie went. Though safe from Jacob at church, I also maintained a safe distance from church people. I could not let anyone close. Too much risk if someone realized what happened in my home.

But was it truly that bad? He had never broken my bones. He had never given me a bloodied nose. Not even blackened one of my eyes. In fact, I did bruise easily. Jacob said so every time he left a mark. He told me, "If I had really slapped you, I would take my hand ALL the way back."

And I knew, if he really wanted to choke me, he would not let go.

Sometimes we had good moments, even laughter, at a scene in a movie or an outing somewhere. The fights were not every day. A few months might pass in between the horrible times with simply "little miscommunications" here and there.

I thought if I tried harder to understand him and listened more like he said, it could get better. He never meant to hurt Millie or me. And he was not that bad with Amelia. He tried to be a father figure to her. He just got so angry at times. But we were all he had and he was so sorry. He cried as easily as he grew angry.

Even though I never wanted to leave Millie with him, he never had a child before so he was learning to be a father. Right? Amelia was not his biological daughter. Because of that, he controlled himself better. As she grew older he kept his temper in check with her. Amelia was always so easy going to begin with, rarely striking anger in anyone.

Protecting my daughters until God changed him and made him a better, safer dad was my job. Stick with Jacob, pray for my husband, keep working on my relationship with Jesus and it would get better.

It had to.

†††

One evening, after a children's event at church, I sat in the office with a woman in leadership. In amazement, I listened as she said, "I left him with the clothes on my back and what I could carry. Grabbed my girls and we fled."

She shared her story. Not a woman of poverty, quite the opposite, blessed with abundant wealth. Or she had been. To leave him was to leave it all. Her husband was an abusive man. She finally ran.

"That had to take so much strength and courage." I stared at her.

The floodgate that held back a wall of tears threatened to burst open. For a long time, we talked. I listened to a woman whom I already admired tell a tale of courage like I had never heard.

She ended with, "I don't know why I told you all this. Not many people know."

I knew. Because I lived with a man like the man she left.

Jesus wanted me to see the trust she had in him. To feel hope and life. My thoughts flickered, dancing in my mind. Partnered with the lingering of sandalwood in the air from her perfume. Did she bring it with her when she fled those years ago?

*What if I tell her now? Could she help us? What if she called someone? The police. What if they took my girls? I'm keeping Millie safe as best I can. I do not leave her alone with him when I don't have to. Besides, Jacob is trying to change. I can be strong and deal with this. Just keep believing and praying.*

"Your words will not go beyond these walls," I assured her with much respect. "Your story is safe with me." Secrets were my specialty. "Thank you for sharing with me. It means so much."

I smiled, deeply touched. *If only I could tell her how much her story meant to me.*

A spark ignited that night. A little flame to help me see the truth. If Jacob did not change, a choice might have to be made. He had a choice to make, too.

*I do not believe in divorce but how can all this hurt, anger, lies, and fear be of God? I have prayed for Jacob, I prayed for us and how long, Lord, do I cover bruises? I am smothering secrets that hurt us. Is this love and submission or fear and control? Is it a warped perception of all these things? Is my faith growing, Father, or faltering?*

Part of me knew. God threw me a lifeline that night but I did not grab it. I was too afraid. Not enough trust yet for anyone. Even God. And there were those ifs. Too many ifs.

✝✝✝

"Where are you going?" Jacob screamed as I backed the car out of the driveway. Explosive, he slammed open the screen door and ran down the steps.

*What if he gets to me? Look out the rear window. Ignore him as he barrels towards the car. Back out as fast as you can.*

"It's okay, baby." I told Millie. I could feel her fear in her quietness. Not a sound. "We'll be okay," I promised.

He had taken a break from his hours of abuse to walk into the family room. The TV a temporary distraction.

So I ran.

*Where was my purse? My car keys? Oh, God, Laney, hurry up before he comes back in here. Quick! Go get Millie and hurry. Quiet. Just go. Get to the car. God, please keep him in there till we get out,* I silently screamed.

"Come with mama." I knelt and whispered to my daughter.

Millie looked up with knowing eyes and did not question. I held a finger to my lips. "Sh-h-h."

Maybe because the fighting had been going on for many hours and with such intensity, my young yet wise child sensed the urgency in her mama's voice. Millie was compliant. Quiet as a tiny, voiceless woman frozen by fear, she reached up and took my hand. We raced out the door to the car.

*Get out of the driveway. Don't wreck the car. Don't stop. Drive away from here. He can't catch the car when you're farther down the road. Don't look at him. Don't look at his face. Press the accelerator and drive.*

Drive I did in absolute terrified silence. No clue as to where I was going: in the car, in my life or with him. I knew of nowhere to go. I knew in that moment I could not take any more. This life was not right. All the things

~38~

he said, how he made us feel. What he did to us when he was angry was not right. I wanted to leave Jacob.

How he screamed, backed me into corners, held me down, and grabbed my face. All the arguing for hours had driven me over the edge. Must I always be there to intervene with him and Millie? Would it get better as he promised or worse? Lies, lies and more lies. All the pain. Excuses and "I'm sorrys."

What did they really mean? How could I ever understand or make him happy with anything I said or did? I could not trust him. Was I ever able to trust him?

Gravel crunched under the tires as I rolled to a stop in front of the lonely lake. The only sound I heard except my sobs. Millie had been eerily quiet. I turned off the engine and put the car in park.

"What are we doing, Mama?" she asked.

"I don't know, Baby." My words barely fell out of my mouth. "I've got to think."

I looked at my child. Rubbed her small hand. I had no other answers to give. She was silent again.

In the quiet, minutes passed as my heartbeat began to slow. The consequences of my isolation and sealed lips set in. All the secrets I kept to cover and protect now damaged us. No one knew. Not one single person on this earth had a clue how he hurt us and scared us. We were alone.

Somewhere, as I grew up, it was ingrained in me no matter what happened between husband and wife, it was private. No one's business. You covered your spouse. Period. I covered until we almost suffocated.

Who would I tell? Where would we go, my two girls and I? Amelia had been at work all day and was not due home till late tonight. Do I drive to her job now? How would I support us with my salary? I still had too much debt. What about all my things I left at the house?

*Oh, God! What should I do?*

No answers. Too many walls in front of my eyes. Not enough cracks yet broken through for me to see enough light. Too many chains around my wrist and not just Jacob's hands holding me down.

This time, I did not hear the voice of God. Maybe because I was so full of shame, fear and despair. In that moment, I saw only the darkness closing in around me. In that moment, there was no hope. I started the car.

When I left Jacob, it was light. When we returned home, nighttime had fallen. Now it was cold and black. I felt the darkness on the inside when I turned off the headlights. In silence, we climbed out of the car. Once again, my baby girl took my hand. Having been through so much, she did not have to ask. She simply knew.

Full of hopelessness and fear, my precious daughter and I walked back up the steps.

"Please God, let him be asleep." Slowly, I opened the door.

Never again did I try to leave Jacob.

## I'M NOT ONE OF THEM

"I'm going to be a better father with this baby. Just you wait and see, Laney."

Was I supposed to bet a life on the words of this man?

Six years later, after the birth of Millie, I held another innocent baby girl in my arms. The fate of a child on my shoulders.

I had no response for Jacob—instead prayers of protection to Jesus. *I know things can change. Our lives can change. Please keep Olivia safe in your hands. Safer than Millie was. And Amelia. Help Jacob change. Please help my faith in you to grow, Lord.*

In 2001, Millie started kindergarten. After another phone call from her principal, I headed to her school.

On the drive, I heard a radio broadcast with James Dobson.

I rushed into the principal's office and announced, "I know what it is. I know why she struggles. Millie has ADHD."

As I rambled about the light bulb that went off in my head when I heard the talk show, her principle—who had the diagnosis himself—smiled, "I had planned to bring up that disorder with you in this meeting, Mrs. Taylor."

Together, with her teacher, we worked out a strategy. I had to be available if her teacher needed me for support. Millie had had a few physical interactions with her peers.

What could I say? *Well, you see Mr. Principal...when her daddy doesn't get what he wants or things don't go his way, he finds a way to get it or he gets very angry. Millie cannot help her behavior. It is simply learned.*

Not a word. My lips were sealed. The specialist I wanted was booked two months out. So I quit my job to protect my precious one. To be accessible to help my daughter at school. I could learn about Attention Deficit Hyperactivity Disorder.

The doctor smiled. "My recommendations are medication for her and informational classes for both of you. Millie will never go 55 but we could get her down to 80."

He had one of the warmest smiles I had ever seen in a doctor.

"Are you sure she needs medicine?" Tears rolled down my face.

I shifted my gaze to his bookshelves—several Christian authors, as well as James Dobson. Jacob and I listened as Doctor Jones explained that he himself had a diagnosis of ADHD. He would like to start Millie on the same medication he took. He shared about his family, his background and his future thoughts and goals for Millie.

"I encourage you to pray about it. I would like to see her not need medication for the rest of her life. However, it will make a huge difference in her ability to be successful at this point."

The other part of her diagnosis I could not accept: Oppositional Defiant Disorder. Both diagnoses were based on paperwork, behavior analysis, talks and information, which for the most part had come from me. Filtered, of course. Millie was determined to be "Mild" ODD.

Again, I was torn. How could I speak? The information I knew about this disorder was what Doctor Jones had told us. It did not feel right. Defiant? She was not. She reacted out of the behavior she received. She was mistreated. All of the love I had given my daughter could not outweigh what Jacob had taught her. I lived with secrets I could not tell, even to help my child.

The guilt, shame and condemnation were too heavy and I staggered. Things not mine to carry—still I carried them. Would they cripple me? Would I be able to one day walk at all or collapse under their pressure?

We gave her the medicine. We took the classes. Trips to her school when I was needed and helped whenever they wanted me. Things improved for Millie at school. The medicine helped. It was a long road. One I walked with only Jesus.

✝✝✝

Several weeks before Millie's diagnosis, I became pregnant. Would I again fall into deep desolation?

Olivia was born the next fall. Maybe this would be good for Jacob. For all of us. Part of me did want to believe those weightless words of sweetness I had become used to hearing from him—words that floated effortlessly to the ground. But it was too hard not to be crushed with the weight of his words. They carried the power to torment, manipulate and terrorize.

I pictured a calm and cuddly black bear as he licked all the yummy, sweet honey off his paws. Collected out of his yellow, round honey jar.

Then the sound of a ravenous roar as a huge grizzly ripped the bee hive to shreds with his razor claws. Destroyed what those bees worked in diligence to create. Annihilating some of the tiny creatures for his own self-gratification.

When we lived with Jacob, we were only supposed to see the sweet bear and his honey jar. But I felt like the helpless insect as it fled the ravenous teeth of the crazed grizzly. With the knowledge it might not escape.

It did not feel good. It did not feel sweet, this year of Millie's kindergarten transition and another pregnancy. I had to be strong. I had to deal with everything. The two-edged sword sliced me each time I defended myself.

"You control everything: the checkbook, money, everything." Jacob exploded.

"You blow up when I ask you to handle something and blame me if what I do handle goes wrong. What do you want to take care of? Please tell me." I desperately pleaded.

Never any resolution to this year after year argument. He controlled nothing, yet everything.

Worn. I was worn.

The pressure squeezed our lives again. Another baby, his "second chance" to be a father. He wanted this child until another bill came in the mailbox.

*When this baby was born, would Millie evaporate into the background? Would Jacob's attentions all go to the new baby? Could this be good or horribly bad?*

The money issues never left. Up went the pressure. The arguments escalated. It did not matter that I was pregnant. My growing stomach got in his way.

*"God, give me strength. I feel you. I've gotten closer to you. I can see you've done things in my life. Answered many prayers. You hear me. But, it is so hard. Sometimes he makes me feel like I am going crazy. Each time my faith gets stronger, Jacob pulls me backward. One day he is with me—listening. The next day, he is trying to take me back to Hell. To that old person I never want to be again. Pushing and pushing me. I pray for our marriage—for my husband. He says he prays. He reads his Bible. God help me know your will. Wrap your arms around us. Keep us safe. Amen."*

☩☩☩

Jacob proved different with Olivia than he was Millie and Amelia. In his efforts to be a better Dad, he treated his girls in opposite ways. He teetered on spoiling Olivia rather than practicing any discipline. Was

Millie's discipline borderline beating? It sent Jacob and me into extreme fights. He had moments of impatience with Olivia. I never felt like he could be fully trusted with her.

Olivia did not like car rides, especially after dark. Sometimes, to calm her when she cried, I reached back and held her little hand till we made it home. When she was still under a year old, she had one of those times and was screaming upset. I turned around, held her hand and rubbed the tiny fingers.

"Let go of her hand." Jacob stated.

I stared at him but did not let go. "Why? She stopped crying. It helped her. She's scared."

"You make her stay a baby. She needs to get over it."

I could not believe it. "That's irrational. I won't let go because it comforts her. You know she only cries when it's dark on car rides." I glared at him.

He reached back, ripped my hand out of my baby's fingers. Then he dared me to take her hand again on that car ride home. I did not have the strength to oppose him. Only fear of what he would do to us if I did. Olivia screamed the rest of the way home. I hated him and myself.

He did treat her different than Millie. She got away with things Millie could not at her age. Good for Olivia, to an extent. I had begun to see several changes in his behavior with our daughters. Would this create a rift between my girls? A gap that would widen over the years? So much brokenness to heal.

*"Father, I pray Millie not see when her daddy treats them differently. That she would never resent the sister he spoils. That the eyes of the child he said he already "ruined" could be blinded to this fact and she would love her baby sister no matter what. Lord, I know Millie was far from ruined and his words over her are lies. What kind of father would say that? What kind of mother am I to stay with him? Show me what to do, Lord. Show me what to do."*

Olivia was a quiet toddler. She did speak to a few of us, but it was a short list. In public, she rarely spoke to anyone.

I loved to sing, which she picked up. To sing meant she was in her happy place. In the grocery cart, Olivia sang while I shopped. Until someone walked up.

"Hi, Honey." With a big smile. "What are you singing there so pretty?"

I returned the huge smile because I knew what was coming. I would wait for little Olivia to look up at the invader with those huge, brown puppy eyes, go quiet then burst out bawling.

"Oh, no! I'm so sorry, sweetheart." The horrified lady or gentleman would apologize repeatedly. "Please don't cry."

"She's very shy," I assured. "It's okay. Please don't worry."

Whether it was Millie or Amelia or both the girls with me, we calmed down our little princess and went on our way. Soon, she would be a song bird again.

✝✝✝

As a recent high school graduate, Amelia was rarely at home between work and friends. I was glad, because that kept her busy and out of Jacob's line of fire. When she was home, we focused on the baby girl in the house. Olivia brought us joy. We loved her. Her laughter took our minds off the sadness and anger Jacob seemed to permeate.

Our family continued to go to church. My faithfulness with the volunteer role in the children's ministry kept me grounded, gave me purpose. I started to build friendships with the other monthly volunteers, even if it was only surface deep.

"Laney, you got a sleep anointing on you with those babies." My friend Cindy grinned. "Every time we hand you one of those screaming babies and I walk back in here, you done got it to sleep."

Softly, I laughed and rocked the quiet bundle that a few minutes ago roared relentlessly. "Hold 'em and sing to 'em. Sound to sleep they go, Cindy." I winked. I had grown closer to some of these women. At least as close as *I* would let them get to me.

Three years quickly passed as I helped Millie with school, through several medication adjustments, and we moved to a bigger house. Because I still stayed home, I tried independent sales for extra income. I loaded up products and my little Olivia. Together we promoted Avon in banks, stores, restaurants, and anywhere similar. Then I added Home Interiors to the plan. I did shows in the evenings. Jacob worked two jobs, so I scheduled around his hours.

The fights settled down. Sometimes I wrestled with guilt because he seemed to work all the time. But wasn't it worth it for a little peace for the rest of us? Everything changed when we bought cell phones. A phone should be a good thing. But that phone was another way for him to fight with me when he was not home. A blessing in times of need. Other times it felt like a curse.

"I'm already twenty minutes late with this order and I'm lost," Jacob yelled.

When I heard my cell ring again, my whole body cringed. He had already called twice tonight while working his pizza delivery job. Hung up on me. Both times mad.

"I don't know what you want me to do."

He exhausted me in every way. How was I supposed to help him? Me? The most directionally-challenged person on the planet. We had bought him the huge atlas he wanted to help with directions.

"I'm going to lose my job. I don't know where I'm going and you're no help."

I was at a loss. "Jacob, you know I'm useless with directions and you can't even tell me where you are. You have the map. Can you pull over at a gas station and ask someone?"

I listened to him until he hung up. If I did not answer, he would keep calling until I did. Even when he was at work, I did not have peace.

*Slowly, slowly am I losing all hope, Lord? Help me hold on. Please. Help me hold on.*

"You have the position. Can you start Monday?"

I could not believe my ears.

*Jesus. Thank you. What an answered prayer!*

"What time do you need me here?"

The Children's Pastor hired me. For over five years I had been a volunteer with the children's ministry. With only five full time employees on payroll for staff childcare, I knew what an opportunity it was to get the position. Hours were perfect with Millie in school while Olivia would be enrolled free. No better place to work than at my church. I could see how God had moved. I felt so close to him.

Sometimes I thought I caught a glimpse of Jacobs's heart becoming softened towards God. I wanted to believe those times were earnest. A grasp at change. Those moments, though few and far between, kept me holding on.

Small hope trickles produced just enough dew to keep my spirit from withering away. Sprinkled with the growing relationship with my Father.

✝✝✝

"What do you think about getting a CD player and hooking it up over the bed? We could play the Healing CD all night like the Bishop suggested." I watched Jacob's reaction.

"Sure. Get one and I'll put it up."

A speaker who came to our church had a CD he recommended. It was full of biblical scriptures for healing in every area of life, and I hoped to let it play while we slept. Jacob agreed. I was delighted and encouraged.

As quickly as I bought a player, Jacob hung it on the wall over our head board. Perfect. What better way to pour the Word of God into our spirits and sleep peacefully? If I heard it play in my sleep, then he did, too. Hope.

Our Pastor preached a message about writing scripture on note cards and speaking it daily. I did that: scriptures on family, finances, warfare, attitudes, healing and faith. All around my side of the bed and at my desk in our house. These cards did not seem to bother Jacob. Four or more on each subject, taped to each other on the walls, there for me to speak out loud.

"I have heard your prayer, I have seen your tears; surely I will heal you" (2 Kings 20:5 NKJV—Healing).

"Call upon Me in the day of trouble; I will deliver you, and you shall glorify Me" (Psalm 50:15 NKJV—Warfare).

"I can do all things through Christ who strengthens me" (Philippians 4:13 NKJV—Attitude).

"There is hope in your future, says the Lord," (Jeremiah 31:17 NKJV—Family).

But to survive life with Jacob, I felt as if I was in a tug of war for my soul and my sanity. Some days he made me think I had lost both. The rope had slipped out of my hands and I had landed in a deep, cold and dark pit. Jacob walked around the top, taunting me.

We never knew what mood he would be in when he came home. On top of the world or down in the dumps. I would try to cheer him up. What set him off? Would I have the right answers for all his questions? Should I talk or just listen? At times it worked. Other times nothing helped. It was a waiting game until he got over "it."

The closer I grew to the Lord, the more resentment I felt from Jacob. He read his Bible then got mad as we discussed what he had read. Another fight over the Word of God. How does a man escalate from reading scripture to screaming and grabbing his wife? He battled his own personal demons—ones I had no clue how to help him with.

"How can you read your Bible for an hour then turn around and grab my face because I don't have the answer you want about that scripture?" I screamed.

He leered at me. "See? You're not as holy as you act. Look whose lost it now. You're no better than me." Satisfied, he left the room to watch TV.

I held back tears until I knew he would never see them. Jacob did not like our tears. More ammunition for him, and he already used anything he could find.

I cried alone. I prayed alone. I did NOT want to be better than anyone. I only wanted better.

Prayer was the most powerful weapon I had for my family. God saw all my secrets. Nothing had to be hidden from him. The Bible told me he knew what was in my heart. The Father saw my hurt, fear, shame, weariness and guilt. He loved me anyway. My church had opened my heart to what worship was and in God's presence I started to believe I could make it one more day. Jesus became my hope. Could I be strong enough to trust him? To trust that something would change?

Trust. Something I did not know much about—only that it had hurt me.

✝✝✝

After a year of working for the church, I decided to go back to school. Already somewhat skilled in sign language, I enrolled in the Interpreter Training Program to earn a degree. This plan excited me. Encouraged to imagine how I might succeed, I worked hard on my school work.

"So when you get your fancy degree and start making the big money interpreting, I get to quit my job, right?" Jacob directed his sarcasm at me.

"You should try to go back to school when I'm done. Maybe think of what you'd like to do with the rest of your life." I ignored his tone.

A great Monday through Friday, eight to five job was what he had. One he had wanted since we met. A small HVAC company where they taught him everything he needed to know about heat and air. Of course—as with most things in his life—he constantly complained about it.

"I'm not book smart like you, Laney. That's why you need to be the big bread winner in this family."

To counteract his negative with a positive was the best I could do. We agreed I was the optimist and he was the pessimist. At least there was something we agreed on.

"I could help you. You are very smart. You could do it."

I had watched this "watcher of people" for years. When he put his mind to doing something, whether good or bad, he did it.

His far-from-average reading skills as he read and sounded out words for Millie. Old enough to sit up beside her daddy on the couch and have a book hold her interest. How embarrassed he was to read out loud, yet he did it. I watched him read different materials, never giving up, until he became as proficient as anyone I knew. *Hidden away in my memory were a few good moments.*

But when it suited him, excuses were Jacob's best friend. His constant companion.

"You just worry about getting your diploma."

⇊⇊⇊

My relationship with the women at work was good. I allowed them as close as I dared. They were the best group of ladies I had ever worked with. One of my friends even came to our house once or twice. No one else did, because I never invited them.

What if Jacob got in one of his "moods" while they were there? Too much risk. They might see the real us. Not the couple they all knew at church. I wanted to keep my friendships. The value of them dear to me.

And I was weary of the fights—the ones that happened after people left. At home I felt so alone. I was not me. Out in the world, I became connected. I started to like a little part of who I was.

Then two years into my job, a meeting was called. Due to various reasons, Staff Childcare was going to be closed. I was a year into college and felt alive, as if I had even more purpose. Though we still dealt with Jacobs's tantrums, mood swings and arguments, I could see a glimpse of the future for my girls and me.

*God, where am I going to go? What job now?* It hit me hard. *Our finances are already so tight. How will Jacob handle this, Father?* I poured out my worry, fears and heart.

The Children's Pastor did her best to help line up jobs. I received an offer that fit the hours I needed and felt the Lord told me to take it. More guidance came from God every day.

When we seek him, we find him.

Within three days after the program closed, I started my new position. So thankful God had a plan for me. A new start.

✝✝✝

"You guys need to move to Colorado." My middle brother voiced his opinion.

"You've been trying to get us to move up there for years."

"What better time than now? You've not been on the new job long and you can check on your schooling. Talk to your Director."

Michael made a good argument. We discussed details on the what if's and the possibilities.

With a promise to talk to Jacob about it and pray, I hung up. That trust thing with God sneaked up on me. The more I prayed, the more I trusted, the more I felt his presence. I trusted he would answer about this decision.

"If you say God told us to move to Colorado then we'll move," Jacob stated.

"But I'm asking you to pray about it, too. I want us to make the decision together. This is a big move."

Too many times he wanted me to make a choice. If it did not work out, then I was left with all the blame.

Too many times I heard, "You make all the decisions, Laney. You have control over everything."

Venom meant for my bloodstream. Headed straight to the heart.

Yet, he wanted no responsibility. I would beg for us to do the checkbook together, the finances. He would not. My husband had to have me available when it came time for blame. How can someone that controls nothing, control everything? But he did. He still controlled us.

"Yeah, okay. I'll pray." He seemed sincere.

Did I trust his words? But he agreed to pray, so I would wait.

After several days with nothing on the subject, I asked, "Did you pray about the move?"

"Let's go ahead. Sounds like a good plan. So we'll do it."

He did not answer my question. "But did you pray about it?"

"Yeah, yeah sure. I did. If God told you, we'll go." He was done.

Although I had doubts, I did not press. I could do no more on that subject, and I did not want a fight.

Everything lined up for our move. When one obstacle presented itself, just like that, another way opened. I never lost faith that it would fall into place. God had told me *Yes, Move* and THAT I was sure of. I had found someone I could put trust in. On a level I had never known in my life.

Within a month, the summer of 2007, we were in Colorado. Surrounded by most of my mother's side of the family. We planned to stay with Michael and his family for a year and get settled. Transitions on this magnitude and life in that setting did not mix well for Jacob.

Even though we had the top floor of the house, I do not know how they never heard his wrath. He had to control more, but there were times he chose not to. Worse for me, better for my girls. I could live with that.

Things got hard, almost too hard. The one thing I knew with all my heart was God had told me to move. I heard God and I lived with the workings he did to get us there. That is what I clung to.

✝✝✝

Aunt Mamie's church is where we began attending. I liked it. It reminded me of the one I left behind in Alabama. Same style of music and foundation of belief. A diverse group of people, same as what I left. The building was smaller but my former church had begun that way. It did not bother me in the slightest. In fact, it was refreshing.

I became involved in a few groups with the Women's Ministry and began to pull up out of that horrible place I was in. Depression, maybe? Some plans had fallen through, a loss had happened yet I held tight to God's words. Different directions were laid out. I saw some light and followed as he gave me strength.

One night as I sat in service, an announcement caught my attention. It was information on an upcoming outreach the church did for women from local shelters. As I listened to the details of the event, I felt something. A stirring, some sense of uneasiness. Then they played the video.

Words that told the story of these women began to fade until I heard only silence and the thumping of my heart.

My eyes stared at a girl with blackened eyes. The next one with her arm in a cast from broken bones. Another lady with blood that streamed over her mouth, her nose bruised and swollen from a punch in her face.

These women were abused. All physically abused, victims of Domestic Violence. Still deaf but seeing something that scared me, I knew I had to help. Somehow I connected to those women. I sat in my silence.

*But I am not one of them.*

## BUT HE NEVER BROKE MY BONES

"Here you are, Ma'am. Enjoy." I smiled.

Set the plate down and backed away as not to disrupt. The speaker had been introduced, so we worked to get the ladies' meals placed quickly and quietly.

Many areas to volunteer for the Uniquely You event. I chose the kitchen. To serve the ladies their dinner was where I felt drawn. Would this be enough to show them I cared? Touch them in some small way?

My nature was to serve. To please. Conditioned as a child to be a people pleaser.

The ladies from the shelters experienced pain. I wanted to ease their aching—doing the only thing I knew—being of service to them.

These women were at this event because they were abused. Regardless if it happened once or repeatedly for the past thirty years, was irrelevant. It happened.

Did some of them feel mentally, physically and spiritually drained? When they lived with their abusers, did they serve them?

How long had it been since these women were pampered and served? Or felt it was okay to have a few hours of luxury? How long since they allowed themselves to feel loved? How many of them were givers and servers by nature? Or knew how to receive it in return?

Tonight was about them, catering to their individual wants and needs. It was orchestrated to make each lady feel special, because she WAS special. She deserved to be seated at the dinner table, treated like the daughter of the most high King. To restore a part of her worth stolen by her batterer. Fully restored if she believed what the Pastor spoke and chose to accept it.

"Would you like more water?" I whispered.

She nodded her head. Smiled. "Thank you."

I filled the glass. "You're welcome." I smiled back.

So many hearts wounded and damaged. With each glass I filled, the more water they drank, the more of *them* I soaked in.

It could be worse at home. Several of them had missing teeth. Knocked out from a prior "incident," maybe? Some had lived in the shelter for a few months while others recently came to call it home. The evidence of fresh bruises as their giveaway. Pain I knew all too well.

Though my insides gnawed, part of me found solace in the fact that I was not like them. My circumstances were better. I was not in a shelter and not physically broken. I did not need all this help. So humbled to be able to serve them.

My comparisons condoned my secrets. Weakened fingers so tightly grasped hidden sins. What I saw gave me renewed strength to grip harder.

I felt their hurt, imagined the loneliness and trembled with their fears, but I could not share in the exposure of secrets. Because I knew they were special, I served them. They were loved. My heart full of compassion and God's leading. That was as close as I would get.

Mentally charged and physically exhausted, I drove home. A connection had been made with these women. Yet something inside still remained unsettled.

*I'm missing something, but what is it, Lord?*

They were strong women. Courageous women. Many of them I saw enter the church hopeless and leave with hope. Walk in with shame and leave in joy. I witnessed God change women that sought him.

*God, thank you that I don't have it as bad as those women. Thank you that you continue to keep my precious girls safe. Thank you for the hope, strength and faith I saw in these women. Please lead me in the way I should go. Guide me, Father. Your Word says you will. I am weak. I am afraid. Please give me strength. Show me what I don't see. In Jesus' Name, Amen."*

✝✝✝

My extended family appeared to genuinely enjoy each other. Was this what family was supposed to be like? Disagreements were talked about in love and worked out. Most importantly, when it came to gatherings, differences were put aside and family was enjoyed. Relationship was the priority, not personal issues.

They seemed to be at ease, relaxed with each other. Not caught up in the battle of who was most slick of tongue and how to tear the other down—with a smile, of course. Or make jokes at each other's expense, then call it "playing" when someone got upset because the jokes went too far. The teasing I witnessed was done playfully, to make you feel included—not excluded or belittled.

My mother's family appeared to trust each other. At least what I envisioned trust to look like.

*When they confided in each other, did they keep those confidences? Not feeling the treasures they shared were later destroyed or sold to be used for another's benefit.*

My siblings and I learned to function within our dysfunction. After all, each family has their own amount of dysfunction. Should I look for someone to blame in our family? Why we were not taught how to communicate? Solve our differences in a somewhat healthy manner. Handle confrontations in life. Blame would serve no purpose now. We dealt how we dealt.

I longed to have more of what I watched happen with extended family. Why did I not find this feeling with Jacob? As the interactions continued with my mom's side of the family, the more special I felt. Treated differently. Valued. My family welcomed us into everything from the minute we moved to Colorado. We felt instant acceptance. At least the girls and I did.

During the first several years, I noticed how brother related to brother and husband spoke to wife. I reflected upon my own marriage. Even took the magnifying glass to my parent's relationship. Began to compare the flaws that surfaced to what was right in front of my eyes.

As I did my investigative work, I had no shortage of relationships to watch. It was a big family. I saw people who were not perfect full of deeply-rooted love and care. When they interacted, there was a certain amount of respect.

Jacobs's perception proved to be much different than mine. What huge blinders kept him from seeing the ways family here related better? Even their children were treated with an extra level of care and tenderness that was new to me.

He began the same grueling tactics he had used with my Alabama family. Everyone here had something against him. He found faults to point out in each person.

"Are you really telling me you HONESTLY did not see how Luke looked at me?" He accused.

"No, Jacob. I really did not."

To be engaged in the same redundant question and answer session, unrestricted by time, was the last thing I wanted.

In disbelief he stared at me. Shook his head, mumbled and walked into the other room.

*How can it always be everyone else? Always my family? A friend? Co-worker? Maybe it's more Jacob than anyone. Why would he want to make me dread leaving every family function because I was afraid of the fights that always happened?*

Sometimes it felt as though he was jealous of anyone else we spent time with. That seemed ludicrous.

Was Jacob envious? Especially of Aunt Mamie. Some nights after the women's Bible groups, we might go out for coffee. Or an occasional lunch date. The girls and I did not do much but stay at home. It created strife if Jacob called and we were out "having fun" while he was at work.

Alone time with my aunt was one of the few things I looked forward to. Our relationship had been formed through the years prior to the move to Colorado but I had not known her on an intimate level. A trust bond was forming. Aunt Mamie prayed, counseled, listened and gave me tidbits of wisdom. She laughed with me and loved me. Most important—I saw her live what she spoke.

"What is it with you and your aunt anyway?" Jacob sneered as he waited for my answer.

My response scratched his fight itching to happen. It was a lose-lose situation.

"What do you mean?" I asked.

*Monotone, keep your voice steady. You might keep this one from escalating if you play dumb. Again.* I knew he meant our few coffee dates.

"You spend more time with her than you do with me." His face inches from mine. "You think you're special now that we don't live in Alabama? You're too good to do anything with me, huh? We're up here with this family now?"

"You are the only person I spend time with. I see Aunt Mamie a few times a month. What is wrong with our family here that you have to belittle them? They've been good to us, all of us." I felt my self control slipping away.

*What distorted his vision so horribly that when the sunshine was right there he would draw the dark clouds in to cover it up? He burned in the brightness of its joy.*

"You put your aunt up on a pedestal. She's not God, you know." He was enraged.

I did what I had not wanted to do. I fed into his hunger, my own emotions not controlled.

Now I was trapped in a corner. Jacob's finger repeatedly hit my lip while he screamed. Left with the taste of blood from my already chapped skin. Belittled the one woman in my life who helped me believe I was worthy of something besides shame, guilt and lies. She invested the time in a one-on-one relationship. I now listened for God and Aunt Mamie.

Jacob had a BIG issue with Aunt Mamie, at least to MY face. It ripped me to pieces.

Tears cascaded down my face. He took my tears, I always tried so desperately to keep from him. They were mine. The one thing my girls and I owned, he could not take from us. He used our tears as a weapon. He made them his.

"Why are you crying?" He stopped pacing. Stood still. "I'm the one who should be crying. I'm the one who has to work while you go out to lunch. Have your fun. You know those tears don't work on me."

Hated my tears. At that moment, I hated him. Then, no more anger, he had my tears. I felt nothing. Only numbness and sadness.

*God, help me. Help me with my emotions because I failed. Help me control myself. I cannot take it. Help this stop.*

Softly I spoke, "I know Aunt Mamie is not God and she is not perfect. I try to share with you some things we talk about. I believe she is a Godly woman. That doesn't mean I don't want to spend time with you. I'm sorry. Can I please go finish what I was doing?"

Still backed in my corner. Afraid but not showing him. *Am I like those women I served at the Uniquely You Event? Am I abused? But he has never broken my bones....*

After he thought about it, I was allowed to walk away. Never knew if it was finished for good. Would he go on for hours and hours or start back up when I went to bed? His pattern was to bring it back up a week or even a few months later.

Jacob might steal my tears but he could not stop what I saw when the tears dried: a different family dynamics, treatment, relationships, trust and respect. He taught me how to be a people-watcher. He was a good teacher. Or maybe I was a good student.

Bonds continued to form with our extended family and my girls and me. I loved being at our family social gatherings. Hated to leave. To go from a relaxed, peaceful, loving atmosphere to thick air, pretense and distrust stifled me. Once in a while, we would have no argument. The old saying "It takes two to tango" might have a little truth to it. But I lived in a home where when someone wanted to fight, he would fight.

We had a few options. The other person could listen and not talk. Then the argument might start, "Why are you not talking?" If we tried to talk, it might evolve into "Well, what do you mean by that?"

If a person wants to fight, he will. Of course we could leave the room. Then, he got real ugly.

When I tried to avoid his fights because of the emotional, verbal and sometimes physical hurt was I like *those* women? Was I abused? Jacob had said a thing or two about "wife beaters." But he never bloodied my nose or gave me a black eye.

He's never broken my bones. *Lord, why do I keep thinking about those women?*

⊥⊥⊥

Memorial Day came and the family celebrated. Uncle Abe and Aunt Mamie's house had a pool so we swam, grilled, played games and socialized. Mom and Dad traveled from Alabama. Mom was the oldest of all her sisters. Aunt Mamie was next. The youngest of the four was Aunt Ruth. I treasured both my aunts and formed relationships with them.

What I did not realize was the trust given to them along the way. I had come to trust my Aunts. The rest of my cousins, my brother and sis-n-law, uncles, nieces and nephews, all the others—I was working on the trust thing. It would emerge. I felt so blessed to be part of our family.

I thought often of how I heard God and obeyed when he said, "Move to Colorado."

I looked around the room and saw change, people who lived life differently. I soaked in the atmosphere of calmness. Peace. Saw with clarity how these people did not treat us differently, no matter how twisted Jacob tried to make me see them. How he tried to separate me from them.

*Isn't that the problem, Lord? He's tried to separate me from my family. In Alabama and here. Make it so it's not even worth the fights anymore to go to the family functions. Makes me think all the stuff, the crazy scenarios, he comes up with are true. Thank you, Father. I am beginning to see.*

As the evening wound down, Olivia and I packed up our leftovers. Jacob and Millie left a few minutes prior, and we drove separately. I stayed a little while longer.

Aunt Ruth had arrived later than everyone else, and I enjoyed the last few moments alone with both the Aunties and my parents.

After quick goodbyes, we loaded up the Rendezvous and I backed out. Right into something.

"Oh, no. What was that?" I asked Olivia. "I looked out my mirror, but I didn't see anything."

Olivia stared at me. Not a word. Out of the car I climbed and even in the dark I saw it. Aunt Ruth's car parked caddy-corner behind me.

Aunt Ruth's BRAND NEW shiny red car. The car she bought a month ago.

No damage to my Rendezvous except for a scratch but her driver's door and quarter panel were caved in. Right where my bumper connected.

Olivia was out of the car. "You hit Aunt Ruth's car, Mama?" She looked as petrified as I felt.

"Yeah, I guess so," I whispered. Then, I fell to pieces. Trails of tears down my face. "Get back in the car. I'm going to get your aunt."

With each step came another horrible thought. *How mad will she be? Will she yell at me? Is everyone going to tell me how stupid I am? What if they're so mad I can't come back over to visit them?*

The flood of tears would not stop. I opened the door. Uncle Abe, Aunt Mamie, Aunt Ruth and my parents were chatting. Aunt Ruth looked at me.

"I have to tell you something." I managed to force it out.

"Did you hit my car?" she asked.

I could not stop crying. So much fear. "Yeah."

"It's okay. It can be fixed. You have insurance, don't you?" My aunt was so calm.

"Yes, I do." I looked at her.

She stood up from the couch. "Let's go look at it. It'll be fine, honey."

When we walked out of the house, I felt my fears somewhat calmed. She did not scream, belittle or degrade me. In fact, she was not mad. In my relief, I was almost confused.

While we inspected the damage, Uncle Abe came out with a flashlight. With his unique sense of humor he said, "Boy, you sure nailed it good, Laney." A big grin on his loving face.

I gasped. Aunt Ruth fussed at him a little. That was my uncle's way of drying my tears.

"I can still drive it. It's okay, Laney. It's only a car." Aunt Ruth's gentle voice.

"But it's your new car."

She looked me directly at me as she took my hands. "It's only a car."

A defining moment happened that night. I expected to be yelled at. Terrified to go back into that house and confess to someone I loved I made a horrible mistake. With expectations of bad things to happen because of my action—maybe even disownment. Dismayed I would be told not come back because I had been so reckless as to hit a family member's car in their yard. Much likelihood to have lost the love I had finally started to experience for myself and my girls.

But they loved me. Aunt Ruth responded in a way I was not used to being treated. With kindness, tenderness and love, she talked me through a problem. She showed mercy. Uncle Abe did not see it as earth-shattering. He saw my tears. He wanted to see the damage. But he saw it as car damage, not family damage. The car was fixable, and he used his humor to help fix my tears.

☦☦☦

Another drive home and another sliver of light broke though my darkness. But what about Jacob? Should I tell him I hit Aunt Ruth's car? He would find out anyway. It only left a scratch on our bumper. Should not be a big deal. But I would have to listen to his remarks.

This could wait until tomorrow. In fact, I prayed he was asleep. I could go to bed in peace after a holiday with the family. Maybe we would all go to bed peacefully. Jacob never saw anything wrong with arguing in front of our girls. But I did. He was so careful to hide the physical stuff.

*If he doesn't think its wrong, why does he hide it?*

Everything was so twisted.

Those women flashed across my mind. *Lord? Again? I know I want to serve them in the next event. Is that why I felt so strongly connected? But I'm different from them. I'm keeping Millie safe. If Jacob gets out of control with her, I step in for my child. He acts better with Olivia.*

*I know how we're living isn't good. Tonight I experienced something I've never had with my own husband. In fact, I have a hard time remembering any experience like that. What we're living in Lord, is the opposite. It's fear, anger, manipulation, control, lies and distrust. I live with pain, shame, guilt and bruises. I've let my daughter walk around with some of these, too. And I hold so many secrets.*

But that word—"abused." Such a harsh word.

Think. I needed to think. I kept coming back to…but he has never broken my bones.

## FAMILY SECRET

When we brought her home, two big round blue eyes stared at me in terror. I was told she was not used to people. She needed someone who would be gentle and kind. Spend extra time with her and give more patience because she had been alone. I wanted to help.

"Come on out baby," I coax. "It's okay. I won't hurt you."

To feel frightened and alone were mutual feelings. If she would let me hold her—comfort her—maybe she would begin to trust. Bond with me.

My arm hit the door to the carrier just enough to startle the half feral cat. Out she bolted. Now I had to find the smokey grey creature with a level of fear similar to mine.

"Meeka, where'd you go kitty?"

The hunt under beds and in closets began. The previous owner said she worked with the long-haired beauty for a few months, but she was the perfect cliché for scaredy-cat. Determined to show her she was safe and would be taken care of, I would find her. Show her how it felt to be loved.

I understood it might be a long road. Required much patience. I grasped on to this abandoned kitten that had lost her family and now hid from us. Trust issues like mine. I believed I could rescue her. But was I blinded to our need to be rescued?

Meeka, my cat whose affections I had won over several years ago, flashed in my mind. I had bonded with, and then had to leave behind with the move to Colorado. She finally gave in and trusted me.

A gorgeous and strong-willed animal. She allowed me to love her on her terms, but I was okay with that. To gain her trust had been worth it.

"Try to be an encourager to Jacob. Compliment more things he does, even if it seems like little stuff to you. Be sure to thank him often." Aunt Mamie shared years of wisdom she had gained from her own marriage.

I pondered her words. Had I missed something? I studied this adored aunt's face. Had I finally given in and trusted her? Not quite. Not with everything. I could not reveal it all. I held back.

Over the past few months I hinted to Aunt Mamie I was not happy in my marriage. Tiny pieces of the struggles I shared with her felt harsh, demanded every ounce of my sanity and strength. Areas I felt "safe" to tell her: financial disagreements, his mood swings, a life issue.

Once again, over lunch, our conversation veered back to my lack-of-love-life. I silently screamed for help. Scared to go too far or say too much. Would she hear?

"Think of things you like about him. That will help you find more words of appreciation," she encouraged.

Scenes flashed before me. Like a Rolodex™ of pictures, it spun in front of my eyes. Bad pictures. To share those images would take too much trust. I was not ready. Flickers were all I would show her. The truth on my terms.

"I can't think of anything I like about him. I know that sounds horrible but…."

My loving Aunt Mamie nodded her head as if somehow she comprehended how distasteful it felt to say these words about my husband. It was done for now. No more words. I felt no judgment when I bared such a raw, ugly truth. One of the reasons I admired my aunt.

When could I share the really scary stuff? The images on my Rolodex™. Did she have the patience it might take to wait me out? Or know how hard it might be to build my trust? Would Aunt Mamie accept my "trust terms" like I did with Meeka when I kept her safe?

‡‡‡

"MRI results don't lie but we would like to do this second procedure to confirm the diagnosis," Doctor Highland elaborated. "I know it's a lot to take in. You went from getting a routine MRI for migraines to this diagnosis."

I felt true compassion in her words. Yet the words themselves made no sense. They spilled out, randomly—like the game 52 Card Pickup. But no one scrambled to help me pick up the cards and make some order out of them. Win the game.

*Jesus? How was I going to win over this?*

I struggled to find my voice. "If we need the procedure to confirm what you've found, let's do it."

I cleared the huge lump in my throat. Fought off tears. *Pull it together, Laney. Be strong. Don't fall apart now, not in front of the doctor.*

"I want you to know we are going to do everything possible to help you. Laney, there are great treatments out there and new ones being developed constantly." The neurologist's voice comforted me. It was almost believable.

"Okay, Emma, I'll take your word for it."

Tears were noncompliant to my silent command to remain hidden. I wiped them away and forced a weak smile. Tried to focus on instructions for my next appointment. Not the multiple posters on the walls that told patients what labs to check if they took a certain drug or showed us what those diseases could do to our brains.

In this office we were on a first-name basis. Maybe it eased times like this with the patients? Put us on a more personal level? It worked.

*How to tell Jacob? I can't. Something else he won't be able to handle. I can barely handle it, let alone reassure him everything will be okay. To reassure me should be his job.*

*God? What do I do?* My heart thundered.

"…Then we can schedule the procedure and get a treatment plan in place." My doctor's voice. I had drifted. Lost in the horror scene in my head.

"Laney?"

A light touch on my hand.

"Yes?" I whispered. I felt like I was in a fog. Someone else's fog.

"Do you have any questions for me?"

Soberly, I shook my head. "No. I don't know of anything else to ask right now. Just tell me what we do."

When I walked out of that office I knew my life had been changed and I had very few people I could trust with it. My husband was not one of them.

⸸⸸⸸

To watch Jacobs's mannerisms over the years was something I learned to do with expertise. Pick up on clues that he was agitated or about to go into a rage. Pay attention to warning signs that he was teetering. The girls and I tried to avoid anything that might set him off.

When the jaw clenched, his voice got a certain tone to it, a way he would suck his lips, the leg that shook—giveaways to put myself on high alert. The problem with this strategy was we were human. How could we avoid yet react to him perfectly every time? Impossible.

Living on the edge was no longer about humming along to the good ole classic by Aerosmith™. It was about not falling off the edge into a deep, dark abyss and death.

Yet somehow I forced myself to step away from the edge toward Jesus and my aunt—to trust them. But trust Jacob?

If those tests confirmed my diagnosis, I cowered at the possibility of placing something so delicate into the destructive hands of my husband. The mere touch of his fingertips would shatter any hope of support, comfort or whatever a spouse should receive. To entrust the other with their disease.

*I'm trying to trust you, Jesus. Praying over these tests. I believe you will never leave me, never forsake me. Aunt Mamie knows about the possible results and she is such strength in my life, such an example. But, Lord? How do I tell this man I will have to be strong for because he can't be strong for me? I'm so afraid of his reaction and how to do this. Even though I feel so alone, I know I am not. Help me trust you more.*

↓↓↓

"He's not very nice to me sometimes." I watched for my aunt's reaction before I continued.

"What exactly do you mean, Hon? Like how he talks to you…how he treats you…?" Aunt Mamie waited.

We sat in her car at the Starbucks™ parking lot, our special time together that I was so grateful to have. I had to trust her. My life had begun to fall apart. Between the tests for the diagnosis and Jacob's increased arguments, I could not take much more.

I. Was. Dying. Inside.

"You know how the family will say to him from time to time 'Jacob, you're just like a big ole' koala'?"

"Yes." Aunt Mamie nodded. Her eyes intent. The air around us thick. My stomach sickened.

"Think of the other side of that koala. The one that isn't soft and cuddly. The dangerous dark side most people don't talk about or acknowledge. This one leaves the six inch claw mark across a tree trunk after it misses its target. Which it would have gladly torn to shreds in its rage." I took a deep breath. "That side is Jacob."

*Did she catch on? Before I could tell her everything, I had to know she believed me—that I could trust her with my secrets.* I looked away, afraid to see her response. I stared at the parked cars. In the silence I waited, deafening to my ears.

It felt like forever before she spoke. "Hon, does he hurt you?"

My eyes met hers. *She believes me? I see it.*

*Thank you, God! Now please help me talk to her. Help me trust her with all of it.*

"Yes. When he's angry, but he never does anything physical in front of the girls or anyone else."

Again she nods.

"He's never broken anything like my bones or bloodied my nose. Nothing that bad. But he's left bruises on places I can cover. Grabbed my face, backed me into corners, held my wrist down…and other things." I searched her face for a reaction. Once they started, words rolled off my tongue.

In almost eighteen years, I had never spoken these things out loud. Never. To a single soul. Now that I had spoken the truth, how did I feel? How did Aunt Mamie feel?

"Laney," With sternness she spoke. "That is abuse. He is abusing you. I am very concerned for you and the girls." A gentle squeeze on my arm.

Collapsed. The wall I had formed to keep everyone out fell. Crumbled to the ground. My compassion-filled Aunt Mamie walked right over the rocks and debris into my shattered world to be a godly voice in my turmoil. I could trust her. She had waited for me as I had waited for Meeka. A sealed-up dam now burst. Tears gushed. She used that word. Abused.

That night in a dimly-lit parking lot as we sipped what was left of our coffee shop lattes, I spilled it all. The hours upon hours that Jacob would spew his accusations and skewed perceptions I could never appease. The emotional and verbal things he did not mind saying in front of the girls. Only the physical was hidden. Yes, he had harmed one of the girls but laid off since she was in therapy. The abuse increased on me, but I could take it.

With a deep scowl, Aunt Mamie said, "You have to call someone. Find out what you can do to get help."

Panic seized me. "What if they take my kids? What if they think I haven't kept them safe all these years and I lose them?" My mind reeled.

"I won't divorce him. I don't believe in divorce. You cover your husband no matter what. That's what I always felt I was supposed to do. But I know I can't let my girls live like this anymore. I can't live like this anymore. What do I do?" I pleaded.

"You can't keep living like this. You have to do something. Maybe try marriage counseling, if you think he will go."

As she hugged me good-bye, I was overwhelmed but in a good way.

"Thank you, for believing me. For loving us."

We made plans for our next coffee date and my aunt— the lady that now held my family secret—also held my trust.

*Jesus. Now Aunt Mamie knew. Would I ever place my trust in Jacobs's hands? The hands that hurt me more than held me? Would I ever want to…?*

↓↓↓

My Rolodex™ of pictures stopped on a flashback from a year or two before we moved to Colorado. *But why here?*

Meeka dashed past me while I lay on the striped couch and watched a movie with Jacob. My heart stopped. The darkness of the room, lit only by the television, cast shadows as she gracefully flew past.

*Oh my God. Was there something dangling out of her mouth?*

My thoughts instantly went to Cleo, Millie's gerbil.

"Oh, no!" I gasped and took off after her.

My fears confirmed, I froze. Meeka dropped the terrified gerbil on the kitchen floor. I watched her paws tap-tap-tap on the cornered rodent. The pitiful squeaks as it lay helpless.

"Meeka! Go. Move!" My words soft, but firm. I pushed her back with my hand and cupped the shivering gerbil in my hands. Horrified at what I might find.

Meeka backed up but did not run off. She was too curious about her new-found toy. As I tried to examine the little guy for rips and tears, I could not get past the trembling of his little body speckled with blood. Terrified tiny eyes stared at me. I was a mess, too.

"Jacob! Can you help me? Meeka got Millie's gerbil."

Still engrossed in the movie, Jacob was clueless. Millie would be so upset, and I did not want to wake her. If I could get Cleo back in his cage we could talk about it with Millie tomorrow.

*God, I pray he will be okay. How did Cleo get out?*

As Jacob walked ahead of me to Millie's bedroom, I followed with the wounded prey. Feelings of dread and baffled at how this happened still gripped me. *How did Meeka get Cleo?*

My other cat, Jewels, never budged from the kitchen table. A gentle cat who loved all things remained a spectator throughout the entire fiasco. Never did I have an ounce of concern she would rush over and pounce on the gerbil while my back was turned.

Meeka might trust me the most, but she remained unpredictable. She could not be trusted. When petting her, I never knew if she would nip me. Her cue that meant, "Okay, enough. If you want me to keep sitting beside you, you will stop petting me or I will leave now." Or "If you are brave enough to try and pet me again, the bite will get a tad bit harder and I won't let go as quickly."

It was still this animal's terms and I had better pay attention if I wanted to keep her trust. Be on guard. Watch for her signals, her reactions. Be ready to protect myself. Her true nature—the part that was still in recovery from abuse—would lash out. When that happened, someone got hurt. This time, poor little Cleo.

My mind snapped back to the present. Part of me saw myself in Meeka. Yes. Trust issues galore and if someone would just prove himself trustworthy—stop hurting me so much—I would love to trust. I saw me in Meeka.

Now I saw the other part of her. The side I was always "on guard" around. If I did not watch her cues, I would get bitten or scratched. I could not trust her around my girls. They were unable to gauge her as well and ended up hurt.

The unpredictable, damaged and hurtful side of her I could now see in Jacob. I felt stunned at this new revelation.

I loved that cat. Animals can be easy to love. Even ones that challenge us. With people it can be much harder.

Could I continue to love a man who hurt me so deeply? My children? And for how long?

I heard the words play over in my mind that Jacob threw at me. *"I don't think you ever loved me,"* he hurled. The most recent dagger I caught from my knight in dirty blue jeans.

*Maybe I didn't.* I pushed back the tears that must not fall.

## CAN I BREAK THROUGH THE ICE?

"The second procedure confirmed what we thought. Laney, you have a potentially disabling disease." Doctor Highland's words piled on top of each other as she began to show me the results—land mines of someone else's trash with no one to help sort the mental verbiage.

With great care she discussed every MRI and test result, each area highlighted that she needed me to see. Explained. Some of which I understood, some of which I was so lost I threatened to shut down all together. What did it mean for me?

"After much conversation with the lab technicians, we are settled and confident that your other medication triggered this disease. You are the first person we have experienced this happening to." The doctor continued, "At a conference, I discussed your case with four of the world's top brain surgeons and a neurologist. Because of the uniqueness of your case and history, Doctor

Robins and I wanted their opinions of the best treatment plan for you."

Be Still. Let the words soak in. Register.

*Oh how I need to thank you, Father. How blessed I am to have been discussed with some of the top specialists in the medical field. In the world! My mind cannot wrap around the reality. How you love me! I do thank you.*

The other side of my brain looked at Doctor Highland and thought, *Again I hear "unique." Doctors told me I had "unique, interesting" migraines. Not one but three types of a skin condition and there's that word again for this new diagnosis. Unique.*

Saw her, heard her and struggled within my silence.

When I was able to trust my voice, I used my faithful one liner. "Tell me what we need to do, Emma."

My hands reached up to wipe tears as she handed me bunched tissues that worked much better. Confident she had grown accustomed to my statement, I waited. This well-educated and dedicated woman was prepared with her answer. Thankful for the first name approach that opened a deeper comfort level and trust with a doctor.

"We have a plan and another neurologist we want you to meet. He will give his input. If you have family who want to come to an office visit, we encourage that, so questions can be answered. Can I pray with you, Laney?" Doctor Highland asked softly.

"I would love that."

I took her outstretched hands . Closed my eyes. Waited for some peace to begin decluttering the junk yard in my head. Sweet prayer.

Two months ago, on my first visit with the head neurologist, Doctor Robins followed through with his faith-based reputation. A friend had informed me this neurologist prayed with his patients. When it happened, I was thrilled.

Doctor Highland proved the same standards in her faith. Though the physicians may not pray every visit, if prayer was wanted or needed—it was an option. On that day, it was needed.

As I walked to my car, her words spun, tossed and scrambled in my mind. The one statement that stood out—"Bring your family to your next visit."

I freaked to even think of how I would tell Jacob. He could not handle change. Bad for him. Even worse for us. Would he ever come to the doctor with me?

*Call Aunt Mamie. She can help you through this. You can talk to her.*

Maybe it was the Holy Spirit who planted the idea. Aunt Mamie was the only person on earth I trusted. God already knew. He was there. I needed someone else, my strength depleted and afraid. Right now, I needed to trust someone else—a human being.

Support, comfort and encouragement were what I needed. All the traits enveloped in those we trust. Jacob, I did not trust. Would he help me or harm me? Yet hide this diagnosis from my husband? That person was not me. I feared I would lose me. Would I ever know me? Find me?

These past several months I had seen how he responded to my tests. Nonchalant and mostly an inconvenience to his plans. My minimum answers as to why and what the tests were for sufficed my husband. Any physical pain from testing, same as my migraines, did not stop his need for drilling arguments. To Jacob, they were just one more of "my excuses" as to why I would not listen to him.

This was how Jacob responded to life when it did not run smoothly, the appearance no longer pleasant but ridden with twists and turns.

*God, how do I trust this man with this diagnosis? I know I have to but I am terrified! Show me. You are faithful. You are with me. You are my strength. Show me.*

Blindly I drove, prayed and sought answers for all my unspoken terrors. Back to work. My day was not done. Strength had to find a way into my body. Into my mind. Into Me.

Parked, dry-eyed and mentally worn, I did what I felt was safe to do. I texted my Aunt Mamie. "Would you meet me for coffee sometime in the next few days? I really need to talk to you. It's pretty important." I clicked Send.

As I slid my phone into my purse, I polished up my face of steel, crammed another secret behind it and proceeded to do my job.

↓↓↓

"Hon, you have to tell Jacob. You can't carry this all by yourself. It's too much," Aunt Mamie warned me.

Her deep concern still caught me off guard. If I messed up badly enough would she be done with me? I tried very hard not to mess up.

I watched how she treated people in her life. What I saw told me she would never reject my girls and me. In fact, since I told her my family secret she had not treated Jacob differently, not for a second. Of course, she wanted to protect me from him, but she also prayed and cared for him.

Aunt Mamie gave me advice because she loved me. We had lived in Colorado for almost five years. My aunt had been a constant presence in my life before I trusted her enough to reach out. Over seventeen years before I told a soul that my husband hurt us in any way. I would listen to this woman I had come to love dearly.

"I'm exhausted from the stress of how Jacob will react." I looked into Aunt Mamie's face of wisdom. "He can't handle anything and I feel like I will be pulling him back up off the floor. I'm drained from the expectation to support him as if he received the diagnosis instead of me."

"You have to take care of yourself. You can't control how he reacts." She spoke firmly. "He is bound to find out and he needs to be aware of any symptoms you might have. Whether he does a thing or not to help you, Laney. We can only pray about that."

We finished our coffees and blueberry pastry we shared, as I checked my phone again. A habit that was a necessity when I left my children with a person who could turn on them for any number of reasons at any given time.

"I have to get home." My voice tightened in my throat.

I texted Millie, tossed my phone in my purse and stood up.

"What's wrong?"

"Millie said hurry up and get home because Jacob was mad. She didn't say anything else. That was all. I've got to go." My words spilled out.

"Yes, go, Sweetie. Be careful and let me know if you need me."

What had set him off this time? Could I get there to intervene before it got too bad? Was he arguing with Millie or mad about something else? My mind raced.

*"God, don't let him go too far. When Lord, will I tell this man about a diagnosis that could impact my life— our lives? This man with his mood swings, anger, and manipulation. How would he react to this invasion of my disease into our lives when he will have absolutely no control?"*

Fear consumed any answer. I halted in the driveway. What would I walk into? Jacob can't know Millie texted me. It would make things worse.

*Brace yourself, Laney and think straight.* "God, help me and my girls, once again."

‡‡‡

Three weeks. It had been three weeks since I heard those words that almost derailed me. But another part of me traveled where it had never been before. Was something deep inside slipping away or becoming more aware?

*You have a potentially disabling disease.* Those words tried to consume me. As my mind wrapped around them, I was not sure what they meant for me—for my girls. How should I take care of me? Take care of them if something happened? Most days I felt as if everything in life fell on me. How would we survive?

Still I had to tell Jacob. Tell the husband who hurt me more than he held me? This diagnosis could hurt me, too. Though after so long of being hurt, being held by Jacob would not feel real anyway.

Timing, mood, atmosphere. So much depended on when and how I told him. As I wondered about his reaction, I reminded myself to breathe. How would his response affect me? One way or the other it would.

Strength. *Jesus, give me strength. Help me choose my words wisely.*

Tonight. When Jacob came home from work and settled in, I would tell him. Tonight. A good supper, a movie and everything would be okay. Aunt Mamie was right. It hurt to hold it in. Too many hurts for too long to add another one.

If it was not for God hearing my prayers, knowing Aunt Mamie and Aunt Ruth loved us, I would….What would I do? The drugs, smoking and alcohol I stopped over twelve years ago did not help then. Why would it help now? Never had I contemplated killing myself. Rather, I seemed to be okay with letting other people destroy me little by little. Till I felt like I was almost dead.

Not somewhere I wanted to be again. Ever. Was I close to that destructive place again? I felt something inside changing. Moving. An awareness I could not grasp. Not yet. Either I was slipping into the darkness deeper or emerging into a light. So tired. Worn from the black that tried to surround me. Engulfed me. I *needed* the light. Ached for it.

Those ladies at the shelter. Was I like them? They stayed on my mind. I saw them, heard their stories rewind in my head. I almost felt them.

*"Am I them, Lord?"*

I felt plagued with the possibility that what Jacob did to me was abuse. Aunt Mamie told me so. Remotely the same as what those ladies went through. *Am I them?*

This was Friday night. Would it be a peaceful evening? Dinner was almost ready. Find a movie to watch. Don't rock the boat. Make life safe. But it was always a gamble when I never knew who would walk through the front door. Hoped for the best. Waited for the worst.

↓↓↓

"Is that really all you have to say about it?" he demanded.

"What do you want me to say, Jacob?"

Desperation had set in. Perhaps if he saw I was listening, his tirade would end soon. Tired and mentally exhausted, it was bed time.

When Jacob came home it did not take long to realize to share my diagnosis this night would not be a healthy choice. Thick air surrounded him when he was in unpredictable moods. Dark, on edge and testy—a few of the adjectives that dangled in his atmosphere.

"Why do you always take Millie's side?" he screamed. "I ask her a simple question and she can't answer. You act like you have to defend her. Then she runs to her room crying because I raised my voice a little so she called it screaming at her. What's with ya'll?"

Ironic how the tension in his body and sarcasm in his tone matched each other at an intense pace. He came toward me. While my brain worked feverishly to digest the level of distorted thinking in his words.

*How do I respond? Back up and be trapped in the kitchen again? Answers to his questions have no impact. We cannot speak!*

*I want to scream, "We run because it isn't safe to cry in front of you. You make us think you might actually listen. We can talk, but then there's that one wrong answer. And you blow up. You push us until we cry. Then you degrade us. Millie's in a home where she should be safe. Yet she is a powerless child in the arms of her own father. Yes! I defend her because I am her mother. If she feels like you are screaming at her—and you are—why won't you stop? Why can't you talk to her?"*

My thoughts were kept hidden. All the words I had spoken over and over so many times, in so many ways, did not erupt.

Words I had spoken during Jacob's many different moods. When I thought he cared and was going to listen. When he seemed so desperate to fix his problems. When he was sorry after he reacted to us in anger.

Those times he confessed how he was a bad father, a bad husband, a monster. The countless times—for all those years—I had comforted him, assured him he was not a bad husband, bad father, a monster.

How I prayed for him. Believed him when he said it would never happen again. He was sorry. He was going to change. I had answered the same questions, listened to the same reasons of why he was like he was, why he hurt us and how it really was not his fault. Whose then?

Listened to so many why's he threw at me. Was told how I could not understand him, did not care about him, did not listen to him enough, nor love him enough. How I was changing and he was not. So that was the problem. I thought I was better than him. If I would try harder to understand him, things would get better. That I did not support him. It was endless.

His mind, decisions, choices and feelings, I was never going to change. I most certainly was never going to change him. Only he could do that. Nothing I had to say would make him see or think any differently. Not me. Not Millie.

We knew that. We just wanted him to stop hurting us.

I was tired of this battle, yet my words would not come out. Prayer was my weapon. Prayer was my salvation. Prayer was all I had. It was everything.

So my feet did not wait for my mind to give an instruction. They stepped back.

Jacob was in my face, his anger evident. "Come in here to the family room. Sit down on the couch and listen to me."

His eyes black and cold as if colored in by a marker. He spun around. Expected my obedience. Rage walked into the family room and faced me.

Without oxygen, could I still think? Was I breathing? Was I paralyzed? I could not move. Breathe. Think.

"I don't want to sit down, Jacob. What more is there to say? I don't know what else to do tonight." I heard the crack in my voice.

Terrified to think of being near him. What was he going to do?

Before my mind could catch up with the force headed toward me, Jacob grabbed the hair on the back of my head. I was petrified.

"What are you doing? You're hurting me! Stop, let go of my head!" I pleaded. The words muffled as he rammed my chin into my chest.

Bent over, stumbled as he dragged me toward the couch. Shoes catching on the area rugs.

"I told you to come sit down on the couch and listen to me. You think you're too good. I'll show you how to obey."

Thoughts flew to the girls upstairs in their beds. I struggled to stay on my feet.

*Please God don't let the girls come down. Please don't let them hear this. Don't let them see. Make him stop.*

Jacob flung me to my cushion on the leather couch.

Motionless, I sat. Silent, I waited. Broken, I listened.

In my shock and trauma, Jacobs's rants faded into the background. What emerged was crystal clear, illuminated by the brilliant light of truth. Eyes opened. I broke through the ice that had kept me under.

Oh. My. God. I *am* one of THEM.

## THE DEFINING MOMENT

What should I do with this revelation? Chilled bones and flesh thawed while my awakened spirit and mind watched from outside. Waited to join the body frozen under the ice for too long. Trapped. Suffocated. Unable to come up for air and breathe. I gasped.

All those years I was somehow paddling above the water, keeping my head afloat. I had been wrong.

Now with the knowledge—standing out here looking in—I was drowning. Taking my girls down with me. What will I do with this awareness that threatens to devastate?

Abused. I am abused. Jacob might act better with Millie because she is now in therapy. He is cautious. More controlled. Concerned he might get caught. But I am abused. We are abused.

One of the brave, beautiful, battered women I could not shake loose from my head. I am her. Though the brave and beautiful were feelings not felt in me, the battered was.

Mentally drained. Emotionally broken. Physically worn. Wearing the bruises. I am the abused.

Now that I have filled my lungs with air what will I do about it? Open my mouth and use my voice or hold my breath and go back under?

After being dragged across our family room by my husband, my words hung suspended. Direction waited in the air.

The truck rumbled down the road as we went on our "date." A date night that took every ounce of my strength to open the door and climb into the vehicle. Pain in my body reminded me of this dark knight I now rode beside and the sleepless night I just experienced.

"Why don't we go out to eat tonight since the girls aren't going to be home?" Jacob asked.

*How, Lord, did it work out that both girls—Millie never goes anywhere—would be at sleepovers the same night? Jacob and I alone together? How am I going to sit in a restaurant with him pretending and acting happy tonight? God....*

When his words registered in my weary brain, I wanted to scream. Wanted to shout, "Why would I ever want to sit across a table from you, eat a meal and share a conversation?"

*I don't even know what that is anymore.*

Did I ever?

Wanted to scream, "How can you expect me to do this when you haven't even acknowledged what you did to me last night?"

Then I remembered. Emotions cleared. Revelation came back. I was still unthawing.

This problem is about him. Always has been. All of his "sorry buts"" were about him, because of who he was and the life happening to him. Empty words.

Now he wanted to go out to eat. That simple. He had woken up to a new day, put yesterday out of his mind. In his head, this was one more fight I should have already gotten over. Period.

Not yet brave enough to let the screaming voices out— monsters from last night hid behind closet doors—I forced out a calm, controlled sound.

"Sure. Where do you want to go?"

My tone gave away the fear I felt. But it was either my paranoia or he missed it.

*Thank you, Jesus.* To go with him, to be alone with him tonight sent tremors through my flesh.

Avoid anything to anger my husband. That had to be my priority until the girls returned tomorrow. My brain knew this but the part of me awakening realized I had grown tired of being so afraid. But what would I do about it?

Tried to move my body away from the passenger door. Make myself get somewhat closer to him and pull it together before my behavior made him mad.

At my silence. At my hurt. At my lack of enthusiasm.

Put everything into a little box and stuff it into my closet with the monsters? All those years I had to pretend. It was too much. To fake the happy and sing along with his radio was too much. Instead I stared at the red lights of the station numbers.

And it was too late. Jacob was already mad.

"What's your problem? We get a chance to go out—me and you—and you sit over there and act like you don't want to be here."

"I'm fine. Just tired from not sleeping much last night."

He swung the truck into the fast food restaurant's parking lot and slammed to a stop. Now I had his full attention—not the positive kind. In my face. Fury, resentment and intimidation all blasted out and shattered onto me.

"We had a chance at a nice night and you blew it!"

Always entirely my fault. But it did not matter whose fault it was. I did not care about who was right or who was wrong. Had I not been telling him for months?

That eyes were opened was my desire. Something changed.

"I'm sorry. I tried but I can't stop thinking about last night. You have acted like nothing happened all day. Now you want me to do the same while my body still hurts from where you dragged me across our family room. I can't act like nothing happens anymore."

"Seriously. You're still upset about that? If I dragged you across the floor you wouldn't have been walking."

Stare at him. Fear gone for the moment. Disbelief and anger replaced it. Did I really hear what I thought I heard? Yes. His hollow, flat eyes told me I did.

So in the parking lot of a fast food restaurant, I unburdened what had been held inside for three of the most difficult life-changing weeks of my life. My husband looked back at me with the same cold, hateful presence as the disease that threatened to claim my body.

Then I shared with this nasty selfish man why I kept it from him. "The only reason I'm telling you now is because of the fear you might hurt me worse."

Unsure of what this condition could do to my health. I already knew what Jacob could do to me. Would his reaction be different this time?

Ironic how his anger ceased. Everything still managed to be about him. A little part of me died inside at the false hope I held on to.

Questions asked. Answers given. He placed an order at the drive thru. Drove us home. Ate. Then Jacob did what I knew was coming. Sprawled out on the family room couch and had a pity party. Told me how it was so pathetic that he was such a horrible husband.

"How sad is that?" His voice muffled as he half spoke into the throw pillow he hugged. "Am I really that bad of a person?"

So there it was. To console Jacob was now my duty, because I have somehow made him feel worthless. I prayed he would not anger again. But what happened to the empathy and compassion a husband might give his wife upon hearing such life-altering information? Why could Jacob not feel any of these things for me?

With no understanding or answers to the quiet questions, I met him halfway. Tried to pacify him enough to keep the beast at bay. Pointed out if he looked at this very scene—right this moment—he might see the exact reasons I could not confide in him.

Emotionally spent. Nothing left to say, I went to the bedroom. Allowed to go to bed without a fight that night. Thankful for the peace to sleep.

‡‡‡

Paperwork filled out, I sat in the neurologist's office alone. Foolish to think Jacob would have come. What was wrong with me to even remotely want him here? I must be really messed up or desperate.

"Why do I need to go to your appointment with you?" He had asked.

"Dr. Highland told me it would be helpful for my spouse to come for more understanding of what could happen and if there were questions…."

That blank stare, as if I had spoken in Swahili.

"Is it going to make me treat you any different if I go?"

*How could I respond? It would be wonderful if this did change you, I wanted to hurl back in his face.*

What kind of question was that? I gave up.

"No, Jacob. I guess it won't."

Then I shut down. Vowed to never ask that question again.

Alone. As I thumbed through an issue of Neurology Now™, I felt so alone. Struggled to soothe the ache. Our conversation had tried to steal the small peace that comforted me earlier.

Not as alone as I was before though. Hold onto that. Both Aunt Mamie and Aunt Ruth knew about the diagnosis and Jacob's anger. They supported me. My faith was stronger. Maybe there was a sliver of hope.

On the magazine page—the husband who shared my diagnosis, confined to a wheelchair. The caregiver, his wife, pushed the chair. She had cherished and cared for her spouse for many years.

Panic seized every part of my body. Tried to stifle. What if I ended up in a wheelchair? What could Jacob do to me then? Oh my God! Who would keep my girls safe?

It was clear this husband and wife loved each other. The writer told me so. She would no doubt support her spouse in the chair to the end. Fear overwhelmed me as I stared at the wheelchair.

My spouse would not support me. My spouse abuses me. I cannot become the one in the chair with Jacob pushing it. He would push me over the edge, straight into a bottomless pit.

The one last piece of my inner being thawed and something awoke. Starved.

The knowledge that brought awareness now fed my hunger. I could no longer live like this. Something had to change. Now.

It had arrived. The defining moment that would change our lives.

Jacob never knew about the magazine article. Too much fear surrounded it to ever share the contents and aftermath. Yet this time fear moved me forward. Propelled me into a place I could never have foreseen. Sometimes, I had begun to learn, fear can be a good thing.

"I'm not doing some counseling thing," he snapped, "With people who act like they care, think they know everything and are screwed up themselves."

"And I won't live my life like this anymore. So if you have any other ideas I'm desperate. Nothing else is working."

From the look he gave, a few things might have happened: he drew a blank in the marital suggestions department or something about my demeanor made him take me seriously.

"Go ahead and set it up," he said. "Who are you thinking about anyway?"

*Here goes, Lord. Now to see how he handles this. Please help this go smoothly.*

"Our church. I'd like to see if they do marriage counseling." Holding my breath.

Dead stare. Clenched jaw. Silence.

"Do it then. Set it up."

My chest collapsed. As we talked about times he could meet if the church did counsel us, I pushed aside the feeling that Jacob had called my bluff. He did not think I would go through with that phone call.

Maybe a tiny part of him sensed something different in me. He thought he would gamble. Maybe he thought this diagnosis had made me act crazy. His ego decided to pacify me. Play along.

*Thank you, Jesus, he agreed, no matter what his true reasons.*

Because I knew I must reach out for help. What I did not know was what it would look, sound or feel like to walk into a pastor's office with Jacob. But I was no longer willing to go back under that sea of despair.

⸸⸸⸸

The phone call was placed. An appointment was in our calendars. Prayers set in motion with Aunt Mamie and Aunt Ruth gave me a feeling of action. Prayers that the pastor would have revelation to know the truth. Something could change. More hope.

Several things were evident: I had to guard my words, keep the secrets, touch on some of our problems, trust a stranger and not say too much to anger Jacob. So many thoughts cluttered my head. What if I slipped up and said something wrong?

Such a shameful line exists between kept secrets and truth. Part of me hoped the pastor saw through the facade. But what if the he told me everything was my fault? That I am not praying enough for my husband? What if this session angered Jacob even more?

Fear of staying where I was—the flashback to the couple in the magazine—versus the fears of what could happen intensified. Stifling fear. But I could not stay where I was. I would face the fear that might save me. Move forward into the fear that could set me free.

The alternative was to be swept back into that undertow and die. I felt worn, overwhelmed, and afraid. Was I going crazy? The outcome of this life driving me insane?

*God help me. Guide my words and my actions. Give me strength when I walk into that office with my husband. Help us. You can change us all.*

✝✝✝

"You know you can't tell him I touch you."

Once Jacob realized I followed through with an appointment for counseling, he produced reasons why we could not go.

"Fine. I'll go without you."

"We can't have that. How would that look to the pastor?"

So here we were. Husband and wife headed to their first session with me getting advice from my husband on the way.

"I know, Jacob." I stared at the road.

"You realize what could happen if you screw up?"

If I disclosed our family secret? Damage.

"Yes, I do. And I won't." I felt so distant. "But we can't keep going like this. We have to do something."

No reply as the truck turned into the parking lot.

╪╪╪

Two sessions later, after accusations and eruptions set off in Jacob, we were finished with marriage counseling. In an effort to bring the marriage to full restoration, the pastor recommended my husband needed individual counseling before marriage counseling could go any further or be beneficial.

Oh, God! How I wanted to stand up and scream Hallelujah. Maybe, I was not crazy after all. My aunts told me I was not. But they were my aunts who loved me. They might overlook a little craziness. The pastor sensed something in Jacob that needed deeper therapy.

Once home, Jacob was not happy about the outcome. Close to explosive, I was given the task of contact calls for a new counselor the pastor referred.

"You call, Laney. I don't have time when I work. You take care of it. You got us into this."

"Don't go to therapy then."

Millie had been in therapy for a few years. I knew it required a desire to be there and a willingness to tell the truth. She was doing her best. We were doing what we knew to do. Seeking change but not sure where to find it.

If he did not want to go nor was willing to tell even a little truth to a therapist, how would he begin to change? He had to want to do this, not push one more thing off on me because it did not go as planned.

"I don't have a choice, do I? I go with you to a pastor because you left me no choice. Now if I don't do this too, I'll look like a jerk again."

"It's supposed to be about us. About change for our family. When I said I can't live like this anymore, that was my choice to change. Change has to be your choice, too. It is YOUR choice." I waited.

His teeter totter of emotions could land on either side with a hard crash.

Would he fall into a pit of how sad, wrong and stupid he was? With redundant explanations of how his childhood made him do what he does? Or explode into fiery accusations of "Why don't I listen to him like I listened to everyone else?" and "Don't I see how my family only calls me when they want something?"

No matter what Jacob's answer was, I knew this. Something had happened in that wheelchair moment. If I could not trust the hands of a man to push the arms of my wheelchair then change had to happen.

Was my husband going to be part of that change or not? Only God knew. But what I did know was the change in this moment—this defining moment—had to be good. The situation could not get much worse.

Could it?

## HOPE DRAWS NEAR

"I'm not playing these games with you anymore," Jacob threatened.

Games? If this was a game, it must be the old card game WAR and no one had won a thing. For years now: not a battle, a trophy or even a signed peace treaty.

No, to play games with my husband was something I never wanted, except in the beginning. When I was stronger, ignorant and had some fight in me. I adapted. Fought only if I had no way out. The battle felt inevitable.

Then it WAS a war zone.

Winning against him was not my objective. Change, permeating my spirit for months, was my deepest desire.

"Good, because I don't want to play." Too tired, too worn.

Jacob's new therapist had advised me, "Remember as with any therapy, things can get worse before they get better...."

*How much worse could we take? Could I take? The girls?*

He bellowed, "All I'm doing is trying my best to find something we can do as a family, but you've shot down every idea I came up with."

"Something to do as a family isn't the problem. The two places you picked, a water park and a theme park, I can't do right now."

Still learning about triggers with my diagnosis, extreme heat for extended periods of time was something I needed to avoid. As I reminded my husband, it did not seem to register.

"That's just more reasons not to do anything together."

*How does a person convince the unconvincible?* No empathy, assurance or kindness for the valid reasons I gave. Only accusations of how I played games and undermined everything he did.

All jammed up in my mind, I heard my husband's words. Some spoken in his "down" place, others when he held me down. All of them twisted and delusional. I might believe some of his craziness if I did not have my aunts' reasonings and the closeness to God.

"Do you think Pastor was trying to trick me? Has he called you yet about what they're going to do with me?"

Hard as I tried to convince him that would never be Pastor's intent, Jacob accused me of always taking up for the other person.

He misconstrued my feelings I thought were conveyed so clearly during his calm moments. Twisted my other words into "You're MY caregiver. You gave me an awakening. And since I did nothing to get you where you are—it was all God. Maybe if I had realized that, I could have saved some other people close to me."

Or one of his most damaging statements, "The more I try to be what you want me to be, the more I hate you."

My body cringed. Conflict and fear swirled together, swallowed up by a whirlpool of unbelief. How could the man I married say such a horrid thing? If he had started to hate me, what more harm could he inflict upon me?

How many ways could I tell him all I wanted was for him to be the man God created him to be? I was too shocked to ask more. If his verbal and emotional insanities were an example of his counselor's warning, how much more would the physical abuse increase?

No winners here among the cards piled up: fear, distrust, darkness, venom and hate.

Holding onto my hope card—Jesus.

⸽⸽⸽

After several months of waiting, the word "*plan*" now filled my spirit. *God, how do I plan and what do I plan for?*

Plan for safety, change, resources—all things I did not know how to do. Change? With or without my husband? His choices affected the family the same as mine.

While in the "waiting" mode, I clung to my belief that those who wait upon the Lord will renew their strength. Through all of the weariness and work of daily survival, I felt my strength increase. Although I felt worn down, strength came.

"You need to call and see what help you can get." Aunt Mamie persisted, "Find out where you can go or someone to talk to if it keeps getting worse. Your girls need to know he physically hurts you."

She was right. I had told no one else besides my aunts and one other person. I needed to hear what my wise aunt mentioned. I would plan.

With my notebook and pen, words of hate, pain and physical abuse from the mouth and hands of a husband began to fill the pages. Sometimes scribbled on a receipt in my purse or a scrap found near me. Journaling was what I felt led to do.

Realizations of what he was doing to us hit me harder than his punches. To put such destruction on paper and diligently keep it hidden, added more awareness to something about to reach the boiling point. At the same time change was coming. One way or another—I knew.

Choices. Make mine and pray for Jacob's.

✝✝✝

"Ma'am, I'm going to take your silence as a 'Yes,'" the baritone voice spoke.

What felt like an hour ago, I gripped my phone. Held by a hand that trembled, pushing buttons. Almost hung up when a man answered. My first call for help, and I heard a male voice. I stammered through what I hoped to get out of the conversation and waited to see if this stranger could help.

But the questions? I was not prepared for those.

The questions had been hard to answer. The next one harder. "Does he harm you with his words? Do you feel like he hurts you verbally or emotionally?"

"Yes, he does."

"I know these are tough questions but I need to ask you one more. Okay?"

His voice was nice, kind even, with an approach of reassurance.

"Okay." I waited.

"Has he pushed, hit or done anything physical to you that scares or harms you in any way?"

The hardest question. I faltered in fear. Hesitated. Will my words escape? Should I end the call? But if I hung up now, he would know I was being hurt. Could they trace my number? Would police show up at my home and take my girls away? *Oh, God I don't know what to say.* Visions of "what if's" blinded my eyes, snuffed out my voice.

The man who heard my silence answered for me. My inability to respond was a "Yes."

"We can't help you here because we only deal with mental health, not physical abuse. That is why I had to ask those questions, but I do have a place for you." The faceless voice asked if I was ready for the number.

"Yes, I am."

While I wrote down the next set of numbers I was urged to call, panic overwhelmed again.

*This step was so hard. Now I had to do it again? Impossible! I tried to get help and they could not help. What if the next person would not help?*

"Thank you."

Hopelessness tried to envelope me. I reached out and failed. Scared to make another call, I stuffed the paper in my purse. The number that held our future. I walked into my Now. Shut the door behind me. Shut out the disappointments and decisions too hard to make.

☩☩☩

Three days that were horrible. When Jacob overheard a call from a family member, his anger sparked.

"Why can't you listen to me like that? You're like a little wounded puppy, and she can treat you any way. When she's down, she calls you. You listen to her and give her advice, but you won't listen to me."

I listened to his tirade. *Would my words matter?*

Accusations continued until, with television remote in hand, he lunged at me. Instinct said he would throw it or hit me with it, so I was quick to jerk back.

He laughed, then turned and walked into the living room.

I cried, but my tears had to stop. He must not find out how deeply he hurt me. Scared me.

In the kitchen again, he backed me into the corner and slapped my face. Not hard enough to leave a print—cannot have the girls see that—just the usual slight red color. And the heat. I felt the heated force of my husband's hand.

When he went out, I focused on the family pictures on the fridge: Olivia's birthday party, our poodle licking Millie's face, a Christmas photo. My favorite artwork of birds and décor I loved hung on the walls to make the kitchen my happy place. It did not work this time. Jacob's wrath stole my happiness here. At least today.

The next day ended with several aches and pains. A piece of my hair pulled out after he grabbed me.

The third day was an emotional rollercoaster. From apologies back to rage back to explanations, I had to guess when to listen or answer. He "bumped" me into the stairs. He was angry. He meant to shove me. I collided with the wall, hit my head then fell onto the stairs, and sat there hurt. I pushed him away. He laughed. As he moved past me to go downstairs, he pushed his fingertips into the top of my head. And laughed.

Once in the bed, I longed to shut down and sleep. He came back upstairs. Deranged words. "I won't stop until you call the police."

"Please stop. The girls are asleep."

He relented. Then he was in the room again to apologize, to hold me and pray with me. He tromped back downstairs.

As I covered my head with my blanket, he was back. He called my name, over and over.

"What?" So tired.

*Jesus, how much more can I take?*

"I'm going to get my gun and go rob a store so the police will lock me up."

I did not reply. What would I say? *"Please do for all our sakes?"*

After a few moments, he went back downstairs. I never slept until he laid down, and I heard the snores. One more secret to keep. Only then could I rest. But how to truly rest while in fear?

The next morning, the girls and I went dress shopping for Millie. We left before Jacob woke up. A few minutes later, I looked at my phone. A text.

Before I could respond, he called. "I know you're pissed off, but I did want to go with you."

"I didn't think you would want to look for dresses. But...you can meet us if you want."

*Please, God. Don't let him come.*

My feelings were not as simple as anger but mental, emotional and physical exhaustion in his presence.

At his suggestion, we met for something to eat. Smells of greasy fries and hamburgers saturated the air, mingled with Olivia's excitement about a school field trip. We listened to her tell how the teacher assigned job roles to each student to be carried out at the trip.

"My job is the city manager," Olivia shared.

"I can see you doing that." Their father smiled then added, "and Millie would be working at the Burger King." He laughed.

"Hey!" Millie reacted.

Though I held my tongue, I fumed inside. It did not take a wise man to catch the intent of what he said. His daughter knew.

"I don't think your mama liked that very much." He grinned.

How I wanted to validate that statement. *"Why would I like you degrading our daughter? Do you want them to grow up to hate each other? These remarks and jabs are why she doesn't want to be alone with you. Not because I have turned her against you."*

Instead as my heart ached, I made no comment.

Aunt Mamie and Aunt Ruth were right. I had to make the next phone call. Had to plan for a way out if Jacob continued to hurt us.

Found the number in my hidden spot and held it. More images of what could happen to us flooded through me. Sick to my stomach, I refocused on the good. Find the courage to try again. I know what to do—right now, this minute—and I can do it.

Another call for help placed from my car. While nausea swam, the storm of what we lived in—the increased violence—grew fierce. Pushed me forward. Calmed my nerves and fears enough to use the voice that would not be drowned.

A female voice answered. Pleasant and cheerful. How could she help with my situation? More strength arose. The call ended with an appointment and relief. Hope.

Had I made the right choice? Prayer, seeking God and beginning to understand he wants his children safe, answered "Yes." Wisdom and guidance from my confidants, told me, "Yes." Would I still pray for Jacob? I would. Did my prayers for safety outweigh the prayers for him?

✝✝✝

As we pulled into the parking lot, Jacob had already lost his temper. From the few minutes I picked him up from work until now. Once in the car, he wanted to read me a scripture. I felt the tension around him, so when my response did not meet his approval, he exploded.

Out of the car, Jacob slammed the roof and walked away from the store. Maybe he would cool down while I bought groceries. Once in the store, I would be safe.

He was beside me. He found me. He had NOT calmed down.

"Answer me," he thundered. "Answer me."

*Oh, God. He's so loud. What if people hear him?*

"Just this one question," he yelled.

This irate man had now blocked the cart in the middle of the canned food aisle.

"We are in a store. I won't answer anything right now. Please calm down."

Unbelief overcame me. He will not stop and does not seem to care about where we are or who is around us.

*Jesus, what do I do?*

A man walked past, paused for a second. He looked at me, then looked at Jacob but continued on. Maybe that man will tell someone. Save me from what is happening. But no one came to intervene.

Jacob stopped the abuse long enough for us to check out, but he continued at home. Raw anger exuded.

"I'm going for a walk."

*Thank you God! He left for awhile.*

I sobbed. All the frightened emotions held back, allowed to release.

Sometime before midnight, more than four hours later, he was home. The same questions plus others began again. If I was silent, he was angered. If I answered, he was angered. What should I do?

I tried for an "escape" from our bedroom to use the bathroom. He blocked me. He was in my face, and then the slap. Not too hard, just enough to sting.

"If you bruise me again, I'll call the police." I quivered and tried to get to the bathroom.

Several things happened at once. Blocked again, I was pushed on the bed. As panic consumed my entire body, I fought. Grabbed my phone but so did he. Threw it across the bed with me.

The power in his arms flung me like a ragdoll.

*Jesus, what has happened?*

Terror. Pure terror.

"Millie!" I cried.

I had heard her singing earlier through her closed door. Maybe she was awake. Maybe she would hear me.

"Don't do that!" he commanded.

In my face once more, though he had allowed me to stand. Felt and saw the wounds from this assault. I was frozen.

Pain screamed down my back. Shoulders and arms ached. My wrists splotched with blood. Did I bite my tongue? I tasted blood. "I think I'm calling the police."

Was this a smart thing to say? I felt dazed. Was this shock? My heart raced. Could I have a heart attack? Was I going to die?

With a packed bag, he left. From our bedroom window, I watched him walk down the sidewalk. He would be back. I knew it. Minutes later, he was.

He talked about how he had stopped attacking me, his attempt to make me pity him. He would never hurt me like that. More lies. More excuses for why he did what he did. Who was this person in front of me?

"I do love you, but I won't be your victim anymore." My truth revealed.

After I changed the blood-spotted night shirt, I eased my aching body into bed. Then I heard my name. He wanted to see my wrists and pray. I held one out and covered my ears in the darkness.

*God, forgive me but I cannot listen to his prayers.*

Almost two hours later, wretched tears fell. I slept with my bedroom door closed. No point to lock it. If he wanted in, he could get in. I did not call the police. My children. Thoughts of my girls held me back.

✝✝✝

I heard the word in my spirit. *"Move."* The morning after, as I prayed I heard, *"Move."*

Such a terrifying word required so much trust when I did not know the exact implications. But I wrote it down. My next step.

It had been several months since I heard, *"Wait."* Then came, *"Plan"* and now, *"Move."*

*Please give me confirmation, Lord. I need to be sure it's you.* I prayed with a longing body and yielded heart.

The next morning God gave the confirmation. A long-time friend I had not spoken with until a few days prior sent me a text. I stared in awe as I read Anna's words: "Happy Mother's Day! You are an amazing mother. Teach your daughters that truth will always set them free." She added, "God seems to be saying, 'Let them see your truth before you move, especially your youngest. Do not live in fear! Just live honestly!'"

No one knew about the command to move. No one. Tears of wonder trickled down my cheeks. A verse I read that morning came back to me, reminding me I was not alone. The Father was with me.

"Yes, you are." I whispered. No doubts.

As Mother's Day continued, it felt like nothing to me. Same scenario, different day. After several hours of the same drilling questions, I was backed into the corner of the kitchen, again. Face smacked. Jacob gripped the back of my neck and squeezed.

"Stop squeezing my neck!"

He leaned into my face and whispered, "Lower your voice."

Realization that Olivia must have come into the living room. He could not let her hear my cry.

"You've already turned one daughter against me, you're not going to do it with another one."

Then he let go. Turned around and walked away. As if nothing happened.

I followed and there was Olivia. He had made me feel and look crazy again. We had not all turned against him. He called *himself* a monster and I had done all I knew to keep our family together—for years.

"Why would you grab the back of my neck like that?"

"What are you talking about? I didn't grab you."

"Come here. I'll show you what you did."

His eyes swiveled back and forth between Olivia and me. He had manipulated the truth with our girls for so long. Especially, the youngest. Hidden the physical abuse from them. Same as I did.

Before it was over, Olivia had gone outside. Left the scene but not before she saw some of the truth. Then fury I had never witnessed struck me hard and fast. I paid severely for that attempt to reveal my truth. But I would do it again.

All I did was threaten him with the cops. Shock? Too much fear? When would I move? No call made this Mother's Day.

↓↓↓

Scared he was going to lose it one day—hit me too hard, squeeze too long or….my thoughts ceased. Unable to permit such words. His "worse before it gets better" had spiraled out of control. Several weeks since that horrid Mother's Day. I felt as if we lived with a walking time bomb.

I had begun to see with Olivia a touch of the erratic behaviors he used on Millie. Pushed me into deeper prayer for strength and wisdom to do what I felt had to be done—make a move. It needed to be soon.

Millie and I arrived home from a five-day trip to celebrate my mother's birthday. A big milestone celebration for her, and we hitched a ride with my brother's family. While we were in Alabama, the text and calls from Jacob had become relentless. I felt his simmering atmosphere when he and Olivia came home.

Within minutes, he had threatened Millie. A hand across her face. Then he turned on both of us with nasty hurtful words. Crying, she ran to her room.

Unable to address any of his behavior, I checked on my daughter. Then started to unpack. I waited. Hoped, prayed he would settle down. Tired from the trip, his constant harassment and the knowledge I had to go to work in the morning, unpacking became my priority.

"The safe is all yours." Jacob laid a key on the dresser.

"Thanks." I was sure to be polite.

He walked out and my hand closed around the key. *An odd statement.* I glanced at the safe, in our closet, where we kept our guns. Mine safely at a relative's right now, along with important papers as my counselor had suggested. *Was his gun in the safe?* I could not check now. If he heard the beeps of the keypad, I feared that would shove him over the edge.

Jacob had asked for the key to be left when I went out of town. One night when he was low, he gave me the key since I did not trust him with his gun. Gladly I took it. Felt a twinge of relief. Before he changed his mind, I was quick to hide it.

Once I lay down, he was there. More crazed accusations and heated words. When I tried to get up and leave the room, I was stopped again. My body now sweaty from knocks and shoves, the feeling resonated. Tonight, I would move.

Somehow I made it to the bathroom, then took pictures with my cell of the evidence on my body and went back to bed. How did he miss my phone in my hand?

The bed creaked as he lay down beside me. I listened to his apologies and excuses. The police had to be called. Now. Before he exploded again. How could I get back to the bathroom and sneak my phone?

"Where are you going?"

"I need to change my pajama bottoms," I lied.

But I took them, slid my phone underneath and in the dark made the call. Not a total lie, I admitted as I changed my pj bottoms.

Terrified, my head rested on the pillow. Jacob talked. I waited. Strained to hear a knock on the front door. I had moved. The move that would change our lives.

## WITH CHILDLIKE TRUST

When I heard faint rapping on the front door, I slid out from under the covers. My heart pounded. Down the steps as light-footed as possible before Jacob realized I had left the room. Open the door. The answers to my cries for help.

Two police officers beckoned me out on the porch. Terrified, I told my story.

"I see a faint redness where you say he grabbed you." The officer moved his flashlight to a different area. "Is that bruise on your arm from his hand?"

"Yes, last week. I guess the marks from tonight have almost faded. But I have pictures on my phone of others and a journal I've kept."

We entered the house at the moment Jacob came downstairs. One officer walked Jacob outside while the other came with me to the kitchen. I revealed to him my secret spot, where I hid my notebook of hurt, pain and tears. I prayed those scribbles would be my saving grace.

Pages and pages, I watched him flip through. Study. Saw his hand hold up the baggie.

"Is this your hair, Ma'am?"

"Yes, Jacob pulled it out. Hope Haven told me ways I could prepare if he kept hurting me. So I kept my hair, too."

He held everything. "You said you had pictures on your phone?"

"Yes sir, I didn't start taking pictures of the marks until a few months ago."

I could not stop my fumbling fingers as my hands shook. It physically hurt as I showed the officer the photos on my phone. My bruises. Too many pictures. My portfolio of pain.

Breathe. Please, Laney, breathe. You can do this. I am going to pass out, freak out, panic, cry, beg and scream.

*Please* take him away. I had to hold it together. *Be strong. Just be strong.*

The diligent officer sent my protected photography to his phone and collected my sandwich-bagged piece of hair. He gave me back my innermost hurts and secrets, spread out before him. My family's freedom or my worst fears. Quickly, I returned it to my hiding place.

He swapped places with his partner.

"Why did you stay?" the younger officer asked.

A blank stare. *Was this a question they were supposed to ask me?*

"That's hard to explain," I struggled to give him rational answers to an irrational question. "Maybe I held onto hope of him getting better....?"

Would these answers make sense to a cop? Are they even going to take Jacob away? Did I not wait long enough? Long enough for my husband to go far enough this time? I finally called…I moved…but did I do it too soon?

My marks have almost faded. Will they arrest him? If he comes back in tonight, I do not know what will happen.

My heart raced. Could they hear it? I swear it was thumping out of my eardrums.

It felt like hours of questions and answers later, the lead officer came back inside and told me they had arrested Jacob. He had admitted to tonight's argument and some of the physical abuses from my journal entries.

Tears released. Through the policeman's list of instructions, paperwork and "to-do's," I softly wept. "Thank you's" fell from my lips.

I watched through the peep hole of our front door as my husband was handcuffed and placed into the back of a police car. Proof to myself it was real while I held a police report in my unsteady hand. A thousand emotions flooded my world. What screamed the loudest?

*He's gone. Where are my girls? What now?*

So I locked us in and locked bad out, then climbed stairs to my daughters.

*Oh God. I don't think my legs will make it. They are frail with fear as I struggle with each step. Please help me get to my daughters.*

Millie was in bed with Olivia. The parking lot light flooded the room as I cracked the curtain. The police car pulled out with their dad as its prisoner.

As I faced my precious ones, kissed the forehead of my youngest who had cried herself to sleep beside the warmth of her sister, I motioned for Millie to follow me. Wide-eyed and anxious to know what happened to her dad. I hugged her and explained.

Sent her to bed with words of how proud she made me. She had been so strong and gave her sister such comfort. Assured my child we were going to be okay and how dearly I loved them.

When I went to bed that night—two maybe three o'clock in the morning—I felt relief, hope, fear, guilt, shame and trust on a level I had never known nor could have foreseen.

*"Jesus! Thank you, Oh, thank you."* I sobbed.

In the past few months, I had found the courage to threaten Jacob with the police but never the strength to follow through. The bitter sweetness of what happened was too much to comprehend.

Eyes closed, I caved to exhaustion. To rest in the several hours I could before work, then an afternoon of court. No option to miss. No predictions prepared me for the lack of sleep and what was to come.

*Was this only the beginning of "Move," Lord? What happens next? At court? How can I feel proud, obedient even with such guilt at the same time?*

✝✝✝

Key in—unlocked. Now push 9-5-8-2-4. Little beeps with each number tapped, then a final click of the safe. Turn handle to the left. My worst fear would be collaborated or put to rest.

On my knees, in my closet—perfect position for prayer—*God, please let Jacob's gun be in this safe.*

My nervous hand gripped the door and pulled it open. No gun.

On the way home from handling the court concerns for Jacob, Aunt Ruth and I had talked about the strange behavior he showed about the safe.

"Laney, you have to check that safe as soon as we get to your house. What if his gun is not in it?" she worried.

"Do you really think he did something with it? What do you think he would do?"

Images of the last year's abuses and how each had heightened left me cold.

As soon as we arrived home, I climbed those stairs again. Still weak-legged from exhaustion but with a driving force connected to my precious ones. I must find out where his gun was.

The always mindful aunt sat with Olivia as I slipped upstairs. She would keep her occupied long enough for me to settle all our nerves.

Some scattered papers, but no gun. Nausea, panic and disbelief.

*Oh, God! Is it in the house? What if the girls find it? What was Jacob going to do with it? Scare me? Hurt himself? What could still happen with the lost Smith & Wesson?*

Not able to control the possibilities of what could happen, I was unable to contain my heightened emotions. I barreled downstairs.

"Jacob's gun isn't in the safe," I blurted out, horrified.

Aunt Ruth was speechless but another voice piped up.

"Oh, mom!" my youngest announced. "I know where Dad's gun is."

Olivia had my full attention.

"Where, Hon?"

"In the basement. Come on, Mom. I'll show you."

As I shot my aunt a "Can you believe this?" gasp, I trailed behind my child down basement stairs. No hesitation as she went over to a spot and pointed up into the rafters. When I pulled a step stool close, within seconds the crinkle of a bag assured me I had the right spot. My baby girl knew where her father had hidden a gun.

*Oh, Jesus. Was it loaded?*

"Dad put it in the bag and told me he hid it to keep it safer. I came to find him, because we were going bowling. That's what he told me he was doing when I asked."

"Okay, Hon. Go back upstairs with Aunt Ruth."

When Olivia was safe in the living room with my aunt, the chatter and laughter echoed. Ever so gently, I eased the pistol-filled grocery bag down from Jacob's ironic "safe place."

*Don't slip off this stool, Laney. If it's loaded and you drop it, it goes off and you shoot yourself. Then what?*

Steady, both feet on the floor, I placed the gun on the stool. All this was too much. I could not think clearly.

*Was the clip loaded? I could not tell and didn't remember how to get the clip out. Deal with it later. Get it to the safe for now. Lock it up.*

Jacob had only hidden it to scare and intimidate me. Prove a point because he was angry at me. The safe door whooshed as it closed and locked.

⫯⫯⫯

My feelings were almost inexpressible. The father of my daughters was in jail. I felt safe, free, and happy yet twisted with guilt, shame and sorrow. A sense of dread with the knowledge that Monday would come soon, and he would be out of his shackles.

The fear-fueled part of me pictured him sitting on a steel cot in an orange jumpsuit with chains. My sane mind told me he would not still be in handcuffs in the cell. The jail in Coxe County probably was not that bad. It was a wealthier county.

My bruises had yet to fade and his voice tried to control me from a jail cell. He wanted me to believe he was suffering and would come for me once released.

But on that day, I enjoyed peace. I soaked in freedom. It had been so long since I remembered those feelings. The ability to just *be*.

If I had any doubts about the Protection from Abuse Order I signed, they were gone. It was the right choice. The peace in my soul told me so. The sweet whisper in my prayers confirmed it. The confidants in my life supported and reassured the decision.

To close my eyes for a few moments, breathe in the quiet and the calm. Exhilarating!

Calm and quiet were not the same things. The house would be quiet but surrounded by fear. Quiet because we were covered in the blanket of his atmosphere and hidden in wait. Quiet when we had questions of "should we speak or not speak?" Many reasons for a home to be quiet.

Calm was different. Calm brought with it peace, relaxation, good thoughts and emotions. If quiet occupied calm, then it was a restful quiet. To breathe out this calm and quiet was the place I lived that day. A place where my eyes saw vibrant and beautiful hope. Free.

As my morning devotional resonated, my phone rang. A suspicion. It looked like a Coxe County listing.

"Mrs. Taylor?"

"Yes."

"This is Officer Dean at the Detention Center. You were on the call list for your husband, Jacob Taylor, to be notified upon his release due to a PFA. Right?"

"That's correct."

"Okay, we are working on the paperwork now. He should be ready to sign out in a few hours. Just wanted you to be aware."

"Thanks so much." I set the phone down.

While tears rolled down my face, fear and anxiety flooded through me. The devotion of this morning returned. At the right moment with God's perfect timing. Reminded me to bring all my feelings and worries to Jesus, expose the anxiety and fear. Faith gets rid of fears. Regardless of how I felt, I had to trust God.

Panic blended into prayers that no longer could hide and fester. Release flowed from my lips, eyes and heart to the Jesus who heard and would help. I almost called Aunt Mamie or Aunt Ruth but stopped.

*"You and me, Lord."*

Unaware of the phone call or my meltdown and prayers of surrender in the kitchen, Olivia had been in the family room watching television. Now I had to share this information about Jacob with our girls. She was first.

After I revised my devotional into ten year-old terms, I read it to her as we snuggled in my favorite recliner. God gave me a great analogy of a trash can and a piece of rotting food to help her understand. Compare them with our fears and anxieties. Then I told her about her father.

"What if he comes to the door, Mama?" she asked. "Do you know where he's going? What if he calls my phone?"

Each question answered until I heard her say, "Okay, I'm fine." I went back into the kitchen, sat down. For my girls, I would keep up the strength they needed to see. The grief and sorrow I felt for them I could release in private—later.

I did not know Jacob's plans, his mindset or intentions. All I could do was pray protection over us so he would not violate the Protection from Abuse Order again and end up back in jail. The reason why we had over a month of eye-opening freedom and why the girls and I knew his exact location.

I prayed he would allow God to work in him.

Maybe vomit would eventually spill out. I could taste it. Millie said she stopped telling me what he did to her because I had never done anything about it.

We had pulled into the front of the house and parked. With the fresh openness in our home, I wanted to snag a moment for bared feelings. I was not prepared for her honest response.

It took every ounce of control in me not to melt into a panicked state of shame. Shock and fear puddled in the floor board.

*What had he done? How long had my child thought I did nothing?*

Tried to calm myself on the outside so Millie would not sense the hysterics and screams on the inside. "What did he do to you, Babe?"

"Some things you know about, Mom," she explained, "Like held down my wrists when I cried and squeezed them until I stopped crying." She was quiet.

"No, I didn't know. What else?"

"I don't know. I tried to tell you when I started therapy that when I was in diapers I remembered Dad choking me until I thought I was going to die. But you didn't believe me." She hesitated. "I don't know. I guess I blocked everything else out, Mom. I can't remember."

"I'm so sorry. I think I didn't want to believe he could do something like that. That if he did, I didn't protect you." I unburdened. "Things like the squeezes and pushes and the emotional and verbal stuff he did, I knew about. But I didn't know about your father holding you down like that, Hon."

Millie was quiet. Her head turned as she looked out the side window.

Did she believe me? *God, I prayed so.*

"But I did defend you. Sometimes I paid for it physically and other times I thought I reached him. He understood. You never saw the ugly things that happened behind our bedroom door or on the other side of yours." I pleaded. "I'm so sorry you thought all these years I did nothing."

We sat quietly, each of us soaked in what the other had said. Then my seventeen year-old daughter went into the house. Unable to move, I stayed in the car.

When my girls were toddlers, their memories were limited. Not now. I carried more guilt, because I did not get out of the marriage. Instead I stayed until we all had some extent of damage, brokenness and hurt inflicted upon us. Before I felt the strength to make the change in our lives to help my daughters. Before I saw we were not okay—we were not safe. My shame.

I had to deal with emotions from my girls that I was not equipped for. A disclosure I was not aware of as my child shared. I hated myself yet cried in gratitude that I finally woke up and "moved."

I imagined the pushing back of tears by Millie. Not wanting to let her father see her cry. Though with me it was a different type of abuse. Jacob manipulated a different process on each of us. He succeeded in controlling us.

No tears. They meant nothing to him. When I learned that lesson, I too, pushed them back.

Pictured him as he held down his daughter. Her father, as he gripped her little wrists and slowly squeezed them. His huge mass loomed angrily over her yelling. Or maybe he was dangerously quiet. Maybe he used a low voice, close to her face. "Stop crying right now. I'm not letting go of you until you do." Or was he in such a rage he screamed till spit flew out of his mouth, splattered on her small face?

Once again, this innocent child turned everything inside. Each emotion: fear, hurt, sadness, confusion, all her feelings to make the crying stop. So the man who was supposed to protect her and keep her safe would let her go and stop the pain.

Many times over the years, I thought Millie should be a little more upset about this or that. She showed little emotion. Now I saw why.

*Jesus, how many times does it take for a child to be physically restrained, to control their emotions before it affects them?*

Tears flooded down my face, and I tasted them. Not aware when they started. I no longer had babies. One was ten. This one at seventeen with much healing needed. The oldest twenty-nine and living on her own.

Eyes opened. Damage control needed. Repair and restore.

The tears had to be dried as I needed to get it together. If I was strong before, I must be stronger now. To help my girls heal, understand and forgive. Their anger, tears and words, I had to be able to handle.

*"God, give me strength for that, too."* I know you will.

✝✝✝

Strong. That word kept being spoken to me—about me. Even my neurologist, Emma Highland, when I learned my diagnosis. She told me I was one of the strongest women she had ever seen. She knew the intimate details of my life which included the abuse. Aunt Mamie, Aunt Ruth, Anna, my sister, a pastor, and another teacher used the "strong" word.

A week after Jacob was out of our home, I had said my goodbyes on a phone call to one of my sisters.

Jo responded with, "I want to tell you something."

"Okay." I waited.

"I hadn't realized until the last several years…you are like this tower—fortress. You are so strong. You have so much strength. You don't do what you think is wrong. You do what you think is right."

"Thank you," I whispered. "Love you."

Words were lost. I did not feel strong. Weakness, fear, and loneliness battled for my courage.

Even the words Emma Highland asked of me several weeks later. "What was the worst of all the abuse?"

"The verbal was the worst. Bruises fade away. What he said I hear over and over and I think about the "what if's" he would drill us with."

"Okay, I want you to remember that and keep journaling. If a time comes when you think of taking him back because maybe it wasn't really that bad, or the girls are missing their daddy or finances—read what you journaled."

Any reason, if I took him back, had to be the right reason. God had to be all over it. I sought God.

Left the doctor's office to do my labs and was greeted by a familiar face. "Been a long time since I've seen you." The Lab Lady grinned.

"Yeah, it has."

We chatted about nothingness while she took my blood. Then she paused with a twinkle in her eye.

"Well, you're looking great! You're refreshed and rejuvenated and bright! You are looking really good."

Amazed at her compliments, I thanked her.

All these people had spoken strength into me, now and in the past several years. They made it possible to continue moving forward. To not fall apart. I knew all strength was from Jesus. The need to give God glory for each step I took. Weariness, defeat, shame, guilt and more stayed close to my heels.

Could they also see outward changes in me? A physical difference since torment was no longer my bed partner? Peace was finding a place in the darkness of my dreams.

☩☩☩

Now I dealt with everything my girls thought, felt, needed, missed and wanted. The husband and father whose duty it was to protect us removed the safety net called love and security. We hit the ground damaged and broken. His family hurt in painful disillusion.

Their entire lives, arguing defined it. Jacob did not see anything wrong with the verbal and emotional pieces. To try and hide that form of abuse from the girls was no concern to him. But all those years he took great effort to keep it private when he hurt me physically—our dirty little secret.

Now I would keep us safe. Would do my best to right my wrongs. Could I gain their trust?

"Your father isn't a bad man. He's not healthy and he needs help." I told my girls, his girls.

Always keeping my poker face on when I needed to remind them. A skill Millie and I learned to do well.

Did my best to try and swallow my words. Most days I all but choked on them.

"I can't help him and we didn't help him by staying with him. He does love you girls but he needs to help himself for awhile. We have to take care of us, and we have plenty in us to work on."

Heart-shamed, I asked them to trust me. To trust the mother that let them live in domestic violence all their lives. To believe me when I told them we would make it through this okay.

Millie gave a quick, "We got this, Ma," and headed upstairs. Past the family photos that lined the staircase.

As I turned to Olivia, all the courage I needed was found, "Will you trust me?"

Came the soft reply. "I've never stopped trusting you, Mama."

## LIGHT OVERCOMES DARKNESS

What if God changed my heart? I prayed against my fear of Jacob. But that fear was not the only factor trying to grip me. Now I was afraid God would change my heart, make me want this man back. My stomach sickened. A vile taste at the thought.

Not one second had I missed Jacob. Not one. Guilt was hard to fight off. Maybe it was a blessing, to keep me strong for us? To help us change? To heal?

God knew these torments. He knew every emotion. He promised to help me through no matter what happened. I tried to let the fear go.

For one moment, I felt peace. Was this happiness and hope, all emerged around me? This FREEDOM I loved! God was good.

The girls and I purchased another car. Millie started her first job while I started a second one. The annual Uniquely You Event was at our church, and I served in the prayer room again. It was amazing and such an honor. Much more of a meaningful connection because I embraced everyone. I was "one of them," and I knew there was hope to share. I had found it.

I glanced at my calendar and saw part of a devotional in red, written before Jacob was gone. *"Since I am your strength, I can empower you to handle each task as it comes. Because I am your song, I can give you joy as you work alongside Me."*

Where I was when I wrote those words compared to how I lived now: safe, loved, free, forgiven, amazed, guilt-free, joyous, peaceful, and hopeful. Excited to move toward what lay ahead. At times total disbelief at the weight lifted. Crumbled chains fell to the ground.

✝✝✝

Last night, I hated him. For a little while—maybe thirty minutes—I hated Jacob for many reasons. Cried and hated. Emotion I had not experienced until now: hate.

Hated him because he was not in this house anymore yet I still feared him. Each time I walked a garbage bag 30 feet to the dumpster, my body cringed in anticipation of a gunshot in my back. Images envisioned of his fingers as they pulled the trigger. The eyes, black as midnight, watched me fall.

The scene in my mind which flashed repeatedly. Hate for the control he still had over me.

Finances crashed down all around me as his voice rattled in my head, "If you think you're so special, I'll leave. Let's see how far you get without my money." Hate for his cruelty and vicious words.

Millie and Olivia struggled to build a relationship with each other when neither one knew how to do relationships. Their father manipulated them, and they learned his model. I hated him.

The pain was almost unbearable. In fact I could not bear it. Could only lie in my bed, emotionally drained and wait for sleep. *Jesus...take the hate.*

↓↓↓

Shame. The struggle with that word. Verse after verse I was led to... *"They looked unto him, and were lightened: their faces were not ashamed."* Psalm 34:5 and Isaiah 50:4-9 told me if we listened and obeyed, we should not be ashamed. God was on our side.

I wrote down all the reasons I felt shame. At the bottom of the list: becoming a Christian woman who divorced her husband. We did not believe in divorce. One of the reasons I stayed and remained in silence so long.

Now I am enlightened enough to know we all have choices.

We have a God who wants his children to live in peace, safety, and wholeness. Even if that means separation for safety and healing. Whether those choices lead to restoration or divorce is sought between God and His people. I pray all marriages find restoration. But we each have choices to make.

Shame. I had to let go of that one. Replace that list of lies with a list of truth of why I should feel Redeemed. Too many times God had confirmed I was released of my marriage. Time to read his many promises in his Word and in the journal he gave me.

He is my deliverer. He is my trust. He is faithful. No more shame.

✝✝✝

Mixed emotions filled me the rest of my workday. My attorney called to tell me she received the signed divorce decree, so I could come in and sign it, too. Jacob had signed!

Relief! He had returned the papers. Excitement, sadness at my marriage of lies. All those feelings surfaced.

After we finished the paperwork, we chatted.

"It's okay to grieve," Sheena, my attorney, voiced.

I nodded.

"Remember how I told you the first time I saw you how tired and worn you looked?"

Again I nodded.

"Then I saw you later in court and I could see a difference already. Now you look even better: rested, younger and happy. Different."

*People can see changes on the outside, not just the changes I feel on the inside? Really?*

As I filled her in on plans for my new life, talk drifted to Jacob. The lies to himself and others. Sad. Had he done so much lying for so long, he didn't know what truth was? Our entire marriage was based on lies and deceitfulness. Why would I expect anything different now?

Maybe I should let myself grieve. Was it okay to feel cheated of being the wife I could had been? Or having the husband I should have had?

✝✝✝

"If you were to see Jacob in public somewhere, how do you think you would act or feel?" The therapist asked.

"I don't know. The last time I saw him in court—a month ago—my body still reacted: my breathing increased, heartbeat in my throat and my hands shook. I really don't know."

"Would there be anything you would want to say to him if you could?"

After some thought, "No. I spent so much time when I felt and thought he had been receptive. Tried to bring him back up from places within himself I think he preferred to be. I don't know what I could possibly have left to say. There is nothing."

"Okay. I wanted to make sure you had closure."

I shared with Aimee the question my attorney left me to ponder: "Didn't I know it was okay to grieve?"

"But this is what I grieve: the loss of a marriage that was never a marriage. I never had trust in the person I was supposed to trust the most, second to God. I grieve that I lived a life of covering his lies, abuse and him."

"But I always had hope it would change. I don't regret hanging on to hope. I am certain hope kept me strong, drew me to God. God changed me, kept me alive and made me stronger. Hope is good. Hope is God.

"I will let myself grieve. For what I am losing that I never got a chance to have."

✝✝✝

After playing tug-of-war with our energetic poodle, Biscuit, I found myself standing over the soapy dish water. Scents of lemons. Smiling.

Stood perfectly still in my smile. I felt happiness. This sweet sense of calm and peace was amazing. Wow! Surreal.

The house was quiet. It was early morning and the teenager was asleep. The preteen had spent the night with her cousin. No distractions to interrupt my thoughts other than an occasional nudge from an animal wanting attention. The realization hit me that I had more than a few "smile moments" in the last several months.

Have I begun to feel safe in my own home? I did not have to wonder what mood Jacob would be in when he came home or how long until his questions escalated to something physical. No more emotional abuse. I never answered him the right way. Should I have answered or just listened?

No more constant hovering to make sure nothing went wrong between him and Millie. No more intervention to protect her. The cost I had to pay. No more days when I could not control my words and I angered him, because I could not take anymore.

*He was driving me crazy and I was not crazy, was I?*

No, I have been freed from all those abuses. All those things: the mental, emotional, and physical abuses. After moments of torment for so long, little room for "smile moments" in my life. I have never felt as free, as raw, in my life.

Jacob bullied me, backed me into corners, trapped me, grabbed my face, my neck and throat, poked my face and my lips, slapped me, laid on top of me so I could not move, pushed me, bumped into me, threw things at me, punched my legs, grabbed my wrists and arms, pulled my hair, screamed at me in such rages that spit flew all over my face, slapped my glasses off and more.

The bully no longer reigns in this house.

No more do I have to wait it out to see what my life, our life, holds each day.

Toward the end, before the call was made that changed it all, his violence increased. He could sense he was losing control. No longer did I believe "He didn't really punch me because he didn't use his full strength" or "It wasn't really a slap because he didn't draw back all the way." Jacob saw I was not okay any longer with the lie, "I bruise easily."

The Fight or Flight Syndrome was real. Times I tried to fight back. Though against a man his size there was only so much damage nails and fists can do. Sometimes when he grabbed my face or my throat, I tried to get him to let go. Most of the time it was like I pounded against a concrete wall. When he was angry and full of rage, he was a strong yet strangely controlled man.

But I woke up to my reality. I realized those punches were still punches, those slaps were still slaps. I might bruise easily, but he caused each bruise.

This feeling burst out of me over my sink. Could it be true joy? Have I now experienced what genuine joy feels like?

✝✝✝

Church was important to me. It was where my extended family worshipped, where my girls and I attended. Jacob stayed connected at the church as we entered into a second year of a Protection from Abuse Order. The church I loved supported both of us.

Panic filled my bones. One Sunday, I wanted nothing more than to grab my children in my arms, run from the church grounds, never to return.

How could I walk in there week after week with the knowledge Jacob had told such twisted stories about us? What were these church members' thoughts about me because of my ex-husband's lies? After all I did divorce him. All that shame again. All his lies.

He had not changed. His actions in court, the boundaries he pushed, and vicious words found their way back to me. If we know someone by his fruits, then Jacob's fruits were still rotten.

During "meet and greet" time, friendly faces walked up and down the chair-lined aisles. Some hellos with handshakes, others welcomed hugs. Grace, an older woman I bonded with in the Prayer Room, asked me if I wanted to meet for a lunch date. I agreed.

*Maybe I would still run from this church. But before I left could I go on my first-ever outing with a church member?*

After service, I waited, as my heart raced, in the lobby for Aunt Mamie and Uncle Abe. I saw the choir director, Carol. After a hug, she asked, "Why don't you join the choir?" I could not believe it.

"You don't even know if I can sing. I might sound like a bullfrog."

"Come sit in a practice. That's all you have to do. See if you like it."

We discussed the details, and Carol left me with my shock. Immediately in my mind was the Protection from Abuse Order. Followed closely by the church people.

*God! This was all you. Calmed my fears, nudged me to stay and made me feel wanted.*

Over the next few days, I pondered. The rehearsal day came, and I tried to bargain with God.

*"I'm so tired."*

*I will give you strength.*

*"I'm afraid."*

*Go anyway.*

*"What if my voice fails?"*

*I will be your song.*

To not go was not an option. Clearly I heard him. Obedience was my choice. Anxiety would have to tag along. If God sent Carol to me, he would work out the details of the PFA for me to sing—if I made it through the practice.

When I showed up that evening, I sang quietly. Scared I might be called out—petrified. Insecurities swam in whirlpools over my head for all to see. I knew it. Still I felt welcomed by the ladies around me.

Soaked in the atmosphere as songs were practiced, voices merged together, blended and harmonized. As I fought back tears, I almost choked on the sobs that threatened to rise in my throat. God's presence in the room was thick. Heavy.

To be a tiny part of the blessing this team created and worship with them—could it happen? What if I had not obeyed?

It was like a dream.

I disclosed to Carol my new secret of a Protection Order against a former husband and we figured out how I could sing around it. Respect his service time.

As I left that night, I did not pass out or throw up. Major accomplishment! I was proud of myself. It was AMAZING!

That is how a "God thing" works. His plan for Grace and Carol to approach me that Sunday, to stop me from fleeing in fear. I needed those women that day.

He cares about what we need. Now I keep walking in integrity as I wait and trust in him.

Stand in those Hope Trickles. Take those Faith Steps. Move.

†††

My girls grew with each other, changed and started to heal. Moved forward. Sometimes we slid back but that was okay. We stepped forward again.

Tears were shed. Cleansing tears that were not permitted to fall freely before.

"Why do you cry all the time, Mom?" Millie asked. "You're so emotional."

I looked at the child for whom I prayed, longed for her to open up, release something other than the anger, hurt and jokes to cover it all.

"Because now we can, Millie." Softly I spoke, "I can cry and no one can make me feel worthless and ashamed of my tears. They don't have to be crammed and choked down anymore. They don't have to hide from who your dad was."

"That was deep, Mom."

Out she walked. At least she had listened.

↓↓↓

Five minutes down the road from the restaurant for my first lunch date with Grace, my prayer room lady from church. Since I had been "freed" in every sense of the word, I was overcome.

Panic and fear suddenly seized me. Tears swelled up in my eyes. *I can't do this.*

The rational part of me knew this woman was no doubt the safest person I could choose to eat with. Twice I had served in the prayer room with her. Bonded, confided in and knew she was a friend.

Yet here I was, so close to the restaurant, tears trickling down my face, fighting a salty flood and asking myself, *"What's wrong with me?"*

Grabbed my cell and called one of my faithful aunts. Thank God, she picked up.

Aunt Mamie asked questions. I answered. Things came to light.

The problem was not this wonderful lady I wanted to have a meal with. She was "safe." I did not have to talk to her about abuse, divorce, hurt or anything I did not want to talk about. Grace would be okay with that. My aunt and I were sure of it. The problem was I didn't know how to be free.

This was the first time I had met someone from church—outside of church—since I had been "freed." Free from covering Jacob, free from hiding things, free from guilt, free from shame—though I was still working on it—free from abuse: Free.

A huge step forward. Reaching out to people again. I was scared. It made me vulnerable and open.

"This is okay. It is good and you can do it," Aunt Mamie reassured.

Parked, walked in and saved us some seats. A booth with sunlight.

Almost three wonderful, cherished hours later I was back in my car. Who could have dreamed it would be such a relaxed, enjoyable time? It moved me forward. I could feel the shift inside me.

Reaching out is hard. When I first starting throwing hints to my aunt of what was happening in my life, I had been scared. What would come of it? What if she did not catch on? How could I take much more? How much more could I tell her?

Then she understood. She told me I had to reach out to other places. I could not keep living like that. I had to get help. Each time I tried was terrifying. Each time I looked up a phone number. I remembered pushing the keypad, looking at the numbers and thinking of the ramifications of that phone call. What would come of it?

The same scenario I battled each time, every phone call I made during that journey to becoming free. My church for counseling, Jacob's words echoed in my head, "You can't tell him I touch you," another therapist for him, mental health, another agency, then Hope Haven.

All the while I almost hung up. Panicked. The times I did not or could not answer questions. Avoided and walked around other questions. Cried after every call.

Scared. But also tired. Tired of where I was, who I was and who I had become. Saw my girls in the same state of fear, and I could not pretend anymore. When one outweighs the other, when you see no change, it does not matter if you're scared or afraid.

You move.

Later that day, I dropped off a dish at church for a memorial service. As I walked back to my car, I saw him.

Across the parking lot, stood Jacob engrossed with another man. They were beside a piece of landscaping equipment.

To my horror, I ceased all functions. I became like a statue in an empty museum.

## PTSD BY FIVES

In his red and black striped shorts, black tee shirt and cap, Jacob had stopped me without a touch. I forced myself to walk again, his voice resonated in the dense air.

As the talk continued, I hurried into the car and drove past them. No one looked up, engrossed in the piece of equipment. Maybe he still did not know my car. Good.

My hands gripped the steering wheel. I tried to focus but felt numb. Hard to breathe. I was upset but could not cry. *What was happening?*

No answer when I called my aunt. *Drive home, Laney.*

Church. A safe place yet not when he was there doing his "I'll look good on the court resume" work. He had to serve another year of a protection order.

Should I text the pastor to let him know when I might be coming to church unannounced? Bother the pastor with something so insignificant? So I do not have to see Jacob? This upset me in ways I did not understand.

Should I discuss situations like this with my attorney for my emotional well-being? She would know. I tried to control my breathing, the shaking and my pounding heartbeat.

*Jesus, forgive my awful thoughts. Help me get home.*

✝✝✝

As I contemplated this last day of the year, my mood—feelings—were rough. An entire year, start to finish, without Jacob in our lives. Unless he violated the protection order, it would be lifted in six months. The girls and I had grown stronger during our time together without him. Space to begin to heal.

Amelia and I talked more often even though she was still in Alabama. With my oldest daughter unburdening some things she had withheld from me that Jacob had done to her years ago. Time to heal had begun for her, too.

God continued to cleanse me. I was thankful. To cleanse was to heal. To heal was forgiveness so I could move on. Be restored and transformed.

The earth toned plague on the dining room wall whispered, "I am not afraid of tomorrow. For I have seen yesterday and love today."

But some days, I felt so broken. I reminded myself God uses broken. He loves me and I love him. So I breathed in and I breathed out. I knew he was beside me and I stepped forward.

"Jesus, heal me."

Tears streamed down my face.

✝✝✝

Pastor Charles continued his series on Struggles. A special guest was present to illustrate key points of the sermon with his expertise in Jiu Jitsu, a type of martial art. Last week the illustrator had been a police officer, who modeled defense moves. The week before him, a wrestler.

Each of these people added special points and connections to Pastor's message. This particular time Pastor introduced the man who would talk about Jiu Jitsu. His wife joined him for some moves they would perform together.

Once husband and wife were on stage, the expert began to explain each technique. He attempted to overpower her, but she took him down even though she was the weaker and smaller of the two.

*This would have been good stuff to know my entire marriage.* The couple had my close attention. I could even watch on one of the big screens if my view got blocked as they maneuvered on the mats.

The husband described each strategic motion he would make and how she would respond to stop him while he held her down or grabbed her throat. They struggled back and forth while using the planned moves.

Panic. My chest heaved up and down. My breathing increased. I felt frozen.

"The last one is going to be a very submissive position. But if you know the technique, there's always a way out."

His wife lay flat on her back while he straddled her. He placed his hands around her throat. She began the Jiu Jitsu moves to free herself.

But the position, the struggle, the watching of husband and wife....*am I going to lose it?* I could feel "us." Saw me tossed all over that platform without the upper hand of those skills. At the mercy of forceful hands around my neck, his body on top of mine, pressed down by the weight, unable to move. Visions of the struggle, the fight, the panic.

A slight awareness that Olivia and my niece were to my right and another niece to my left. My cousins had stepped out with their grandchild. No adults. I felt alone. Fought back tears that were already falling and an urge to flee. Unable to explain what was happening to me, I did not want the children to see my cry. So alone.

The couple left the stage, and Pastor Charles continued his sermon. If I stood up to go to the restroom, would it draw more attention? Tried so hard to dry my eyes. As I held my head down, the numbness in my body persisted. Numb and having a hard time breathing. Why had this happened again?

*Lord, help me get this under control. Help me with this fear, this hurt, this pain. I give it to you. Please take it.*

Somehow I calmed down enough to hear the preacher. His words about panic filled the room. How panic can force us to react in a good way or a bad way. That we can overcome panic with faith and trust. All the while, I was fighting a HUGE battle with panic.

In that moment, through the vile anxiety that gripped me, God spoke a beautiful message about faith and trust, how our panic and pain could help us overcome struggles. Had I run, I would have missed those words.

Our struggles make us stronger. I would become stronger.

*Was I healed?* I did not know. *Was I stronger?* Yes, I was! I made it through a struggle that night. A powerful spiritual, emotional and physical struggle. Walked right through it with a man who spoke the word of God each moment of the way.

↓↓↓

Two days until he would be free. To walk up to us at church. Sit a row behind us. Attend the same service. Do his serving as an usher all three services if he chose. For no other reason than to watch us.

Free to come up to my front door. Free to do exactly as he pleased, to an extent, but free all the same.

So I took the PFA's out of my purse. Set them on the bedside table. Once settled in bed, I looked at them. Was the date through tomorrow? Or up to that date? As I looked at two separate protection orders, I found my answer. It was through tomorrow at 11:59 p.m.

For two years I had been protected by those papers. Carried with me every time I left the house. Kept a copy in my car. My job, the girls' school, my church— all the recommended places. Each time I swapped a purse, the papers came along. They represented safety, comfort, protection, security and freedom.

Now they lay in a pile, on the floor, beside my bed. Now they meant nothing.

"How can I make it through this?" Sleep stole the answer.

↓↓↓

The last day. My morning started off with a business appointment that tested my nerves and left me raw. Computers shut down, I was given incorrect information. But it busied me and kept my mind off the "Last Day" for a few hours. Made it home, brought a headache with my frustrations. My youngest and I decided what to do with the rest of our afternoon.

To the mall for returns and errands. My headache started to fade as we discussed shopping strategies. The meaning of this day lingered in the back of my mind. Jacob would be free. Free!

Olivia and I took back a refund, did some window shopping and ended up with a purse purchase for me. Not in the plan. As we walked to the car, I realized what happened.

"Do you want to hear the therapist part of me analyze what I just did?"

She grinned, "Not really."

"I made an 'I am having extremely high anxiety today so I made an impulse purchase instead of dealing with my emotions' moment."

An intelligent and mature child, we talked about this being the last day of the protection order.

With a twinkle in her eye and a surety of cuteness, she said, "Well, I'm stressed too. So does that mean I can go buy something next?"

While I chuckled at her humor, we drove to our next stop.

As we shopped in the next store, my mind started to wander. Wanted to speed us up. Get what we needed. Get home. What if he did not understand the PFA was until the end of the day? What if we ran into him? He would plan to meet us on purpose. The logical part of me said slow down, take your time and enjoy your last day of freedom. Relax. Enjoy.

But I could not. Fear was creeping in. We had filled the day with fun, but my anxiety rose regardless. The fear, the unknown and the what ifs. I needed to get home.

*God, help me keep it together. Help this fear and panic not overpower me.*

Another struggle. I wanted to come out of this battle stronger, not weaker. Not let the panic overwhelm but push me into my faith and trust in my Father. That was the key.

Home safe and sound, I contemplated my purse purchase. How would I make up that money? As Olivia relaxed in the family room to watch her shows, I finished up in the kitchen. Then I did what I knew overcame so many things, so many times. I worshipped.

With my worship came awareness. No longer would I look at this day as my last day of being free. Tomorrow would be another level of freedom God would bring me through. "Olivia, my purse purchase has been renamed

'I've been set free at another level purchase.'" I would not feel guilty about it anymore.

Even though I no longer had papers to carry with me, I had God. He was my refuge and my strength, my strong tower. He was my protector with an army of angels surrounding my girls and me. He went before me and he stood behind me. He was my God.

✝✝✝

Would Jacob be at church with his new wife? Would he be ushering people to their seats? Little thoughts crept in and tried to create fear. If my aunt, uncle and cousins were not going to church that night, I would not either.

It was my choice on whether I felt safe for Olivia and me to go. To be in the same church with my abusive ex-husband for the first time in two years without a Protection Order.

My family was going, so I prepared for church. Me and the voices in my head. Both challenged, as I decided who I would listen to. The one that told me what "the ex" might do or the one that told me I can do all things through Christ who strengthens me. He leads me beside the still waters. I will trust in him. I am not afraid.

Breathe in, breathe out. Try to trust. Take a moment, pray and breathe.

On the drive to church, I looked over at Olivia and held out my hand. "Let's pray."

Without hesitation, she took my hand. Such trust. My heart melted.

"Do you know what I want to pray about? What I'm thinking?"

"Yes. Him being at church tonight."

Smiles to each other sweetened our talk. Then a prayer sealed our restlessness. We could do this.

When I drove into the church parking lot, I found myself scanning. Did I see Jacob's truck? No clue what his wife drove. What if they came in her vehicle?

*Stop, Laney. Get control. Breathe. Park.*

I saw my cousins, so that gave me an added sense of security. "Olivia, there's Elliot and Dee getting out of their car. Let's catch up to them."

Now self-talk: *Get your stuff. Purse. Coffee. Lock the car. Get inside the church.*

A pleasant greeter held the glass door as we stepped into the lobby. For a moment my eyes focused on the beautiful artwork that hung against the back wall. A three-dimensional cross to remind me, us, that I was bought back. I was made valuable again. Redeemed.

Inside the sanctuary, I saw Aunt Mamie and sat in front of her with my cousins and Olivia. Service was about to start. Oh, no! I needed to go back to the lobby and purchase my banquet tickets for next week. Tonight was the last chance to buy them.

Funny how I thought I had it all together on the outside, but my body gave it away. As I wrote out the check for tickets, my hand shook. I was alone in the lobby. Other people lingered around, but not my family. Only me. The need to rush tried to overwhelm me.

*I am not certain whether he is here or not. What if he comes up to me?*

The rational ramblings tried to collide with my hidden hysteria. I stared at my shaking hand. Could the ticket lady see it? If she noticed, nothing was said. I made it back to my seat as the music began. Collision avoided.

No sighting of Jacob. One last thought. I leaned in to my cousin's ear.

"Would you look down the aisles and see if he is ushering?"

Dee looked around. Shook her head. All was clear. I felt some relief. Continued to sing, but everything caught my attention. This person walked past. That one moved over an aisle. Another one behind me sat down.

*Oh, Lord....*

Pastor was finishing up the series on Struggles. How perfect. He preached me through. Again. Felt the deep breaths I took in: keeping control, my chest rising slowly, falling deeply. Inhale. Exhale.

My foot with its regular little shakes as I crossed my legs. Again, then again.

I could not do church this way. I knew this was a huge step for me that night, but I did NOT want to live this struggle over and over. Did not want to react in fear and panic, unable to half focus on preaching or praise and worship because the man who tormented me for so many years might be here.

I wanted to be free. I was free.

Worship came. Nothing mattered anymore. It was God and me. As the worship leader closed in prayer, desperately I agreed, "Yes, Lord. I want to see your goodness."

‡‡‡

During the past few years I had taken many steps forward. Came so far. But something I had not anticipated, waited.

The man who abused and victimized me during most of our nineteen year relationship—the man I called husband and father of my children—now had been lifted from his two year protection order. Within two weeks, he began attending during our service time.

Why could he not attend at his usual time? Because it was still about control and intimidation.

After service was over the family hung out in the lobby and socialized. People sat at the square, black tables and chatted over leftover coffee or other drinks. Some chose to hang out in the neutral colored love seats and cushy chairs. The air filled with blended perfumes and sounds of talk and laughter.

My cousin and I went to the restroom. As we came out, the very thing I had tried to avoid happened: Jacob and I walked right past each other. Our eyes met.

Changes flooded my body. My heartbeat in my ears, panic. I felt cornered yet my feet kept moving me forward.

When Dee and I joined the rest of the family, they were discussing dinner plans. Where did we want to eat? Fighting for control, I could not make sense of their gibberish. *Too much talk.* Talk that was fading away. *Where was he now?* Too many people. *Why was I sweating so badly? So hot. Cannot breathe. I had to stop this.*

"What?" *Did someone speak to me?*

"The Pizza Place, Laney. That's where everyone wants to eat. Is that okay with you?" Aunt Mamie asked.

"Yeah, okay. I have to get out of here. I'll meet you there."

Olivia rode with her cousin so I had the car to myself. Prayed. Fought for control while out of control. A hard fight. Something felt wrong. So numb. Breathing would not slow down.

*God, what do I do?*

At the Pizza Place. Checked to make sure the car was in park. Grabbed my purse. Keys. Had to get in there with my daughter. My cousins, my aunt and uncle. My family. My safety. Before I lost my mind or whatever was happening to me.

"We wondered if you got lost again." Uncle Abe poked at my sense of directions.

"Ha-ha, always the comedian." I forced a response.

As I tried to focus on the menu, all I could see were Jacob's eyes. All I could hear was chatter around me. Their words meant nothing. My body, still numb, was shutting out everything around me.

"Laney?"

*Somewhere in this fog, did I hear my name?*

"Laney?"

A touch on my hand. Aunt Mamie stared at me. "Yes?"

"I asked if you knew what you wanted yet. Are you ready to order?"

"Yes, I'll get the veggie pizza."

Then his eyes were back. Somewhere between then and the "Mama, did you hear me?" or other questions here and there I could not answer, it was all too much. My heart was going to explode out of my chest. How could I feel the pounding when I was so numb?

No one had a voice. Drowned out as everything merged into white. I felt as if I might go watch us from overhead. Suspended from the ceiling would be nice. Quiet. Safe. No eyes there.

"I'm sorry." I stood and pushed my chair out. "I'm so sorry. I can't do this."

*Restroom. Oh God, where is the restroom?*

Bolted from the table like a psycho woman. Tears gushed. Find the bathroom. Was I having a mental breakdown?

The yellow sign: Women. *Thank you Jesus, I see it.*

Now get in the restroom and fall apart or pull it together or whatever it is that you're going to do.

Empty stalls and easy access. With my bottom on a toilet seat and my head in my hands, I sobbed.

*What happened? Jesus, am I losing my mind?*

Slowly, I felt the fuzziness lift and panic fade. Began to think my pulse might once again beat like that of a normal person. Voices no longer distant jargon.

"Laney?"

"Yes?"

"Thought I'd check on you, Hon. Are you okay?" Aunt Mamie's concerned voice echoed.

With a wad of toilet paper and smeared liner, I opened the stall, "I think I am now. Something happened because I passed Jacob in the hallway at church tonight. Now he is at our service, and he was so close."

While I explained to her what happened and how I almost lost touch with reality, I felt as if Jacob snatched the chains and clasped the cuffs around my wrists again. Control over my life was back in his hands.

↓↓↓

Six months earlier, my therapist and I agreed PTSD was not an issue. We dismissed it. Still it blasted me out of nowhere, left me horribly violated. Once again, my life out of control. Post-traumatic stress disorder.

Here I was with a useless piece of paper, a worthless protection from abuse order with a scrambled up body doing things that seemed impossible to predict or anticipate. Left with anger and terror somehow intertwined.

I remembered the Jiu Jitsu couple during Pastor's sermon. What happened in that restaurant was much worse. I had to stand on the word God gave me. I wanted to embrace this new season in our lives. Not just about Jacob freed from the protection order but me being free as well. Freedom was not in a paper or an invisible line Jacob could not cross. I had to cling to that truth. What would freedom fully entail?

My life had been shaken. The ex-husband was now in my real world and sent me to another level. My next therapist enlightened me on PTSD and why I lost all control.

A transition from Acute Anxiety Disorder to Post Dramatic Stress Disorder was not something I had foreseen as I moved toward joy and happiness.

*But this isn't the level I anticipated, Lord. You told me this would be a new level of freedom. This is the anxiety I was already battling and multiplied. I still believe you. I just didn't see this coming.*

I refuse to claim this PTSD. Instead, I claim God's healing. I will learn everything I can to empower myself, my girls and others, because I CANNOT live like this. I want this new level of freedom my God promised me in this season he said I had entered in.

✝✝✝

In the LifeWay Christian™ store with my aunt, I searched for the newest thing. Bracelets, my favorite piece of jewelry. I hoped to find that perfect piece.

One of the suggestions to help work through an attack was to keep an object with you at all times that had no connection to the trauma. When symptoms began, you grounded yourself with the use of the object. No one was aware of what you were doing as you gained back control that might be slipping away.

Katelyn, my current therapist, gave me examples of a stone or a coin to rub or a ring to twist on my finger. Because of my fondness for bracelets, I knew what my object would be. The hunt was on to find this new, unconventional BFF.

It caught my eye. A silver chained bracelet with a round dangle attached. On the inside of the dangle was a tiny mustard seed. Around the glass enclosure, inscribed into the silver were the words, "All things are possible."

Could I have found a more perfect object to focus on when my whole world started to disappear? All I needed was the faith of a mustard seed. To rub that tiny seed and remember with Jesus all things are possible.

"Aunt Mamie, I believe I found it." I waved her over.

"Well, I would say you did, Hon."

‡‡‡

I sang through my panic. Sang through the thumping of my heart. Through claustrophobia and his face as it taunted my vision. 5-5-5—what I named it, the

Mindfulness exercises my therapist gave me. They called it Five Senses. What are five things you can see? What are four things you can smell? Three things you hear? Two you feel? One you taste?

On stage, as I stood beside the choir members I had grown to love, not one knew what I was doing. That was the beauty of my 5-5-5. Though I felt safe, there was Jacob. He walked around the sanctuary, serving as an usher. He hesitated and made eye contact.

Hands trembled, breath was heavy and my thoughts raced. Get control. Keep singing. *What are five things you see? I see the lights in the ceiling...breathe. I see the microphone stand...breathe out. I see Carol...sing. I see people...rub your bracelet. I see the keyboard... sing.*

Rubbing that smallest of seeds or engaging in a round of 5-5-5, kept me doing what I loved. Stopped the detachment that tried to engulf me. I was not crazy, not then and not now. Fought to be able to sing against my own monsters of unworthiness and shame. I would not give up without a battle.

I had gained some knowledge on calming and breathing techniques. Learned what the jobs of the amygdale and hippocampus are in my brain. Discovered attacks would not kill me though it felt like it. Most important, there was hope. No one had to live this way. A person could get better.

Great news. *Because, Lord, I cannot live in this bondage.*

┼┼┼

On the way to church, Olivia and I discussed what would be different that evening. Her father should not be there. Four days prior, he had agreed in court to no longer come to our service due to the effects it had on Olivia.

As we chatted, the word "lighter" came up. For the first time in months we both admitted some heaviness was gone. Our place to feel safe, felt a little safer again.

This week's message was titled "Go Home: Healing and Restoration of the Hurting." It was about things that might be keeping us on our mat, crippled so to speak. If we were paralyzed, burdened, among other things then this was the Condition. We learned Steps to Healing and Wholeness and the Way Home.

What resonated was this truth: pick up your mat and take control of this thing that has defined and controlled you. Then, Go Home. Remember where you belong.

Pastor began to pray. *Am I crippled by something, Father? Do I have a mat I'm lying on?*

A worship song began, and I lifted my hands.

*I need to pick up my mat and give to you. What is it, Lord?*

*Fear.* My Father's voice.

The mat I laid paralyzed upon was fear. *Okay, Lord.*

Somehow I was not shocked, knew it in my spirit. I had needed to hear it from my Father. Prayers, songs and worship escaped interchangeably.

*Lord, I lift up this mat that cripples me. I don't want this fear. This torment! This pain! I don't want PTSD. I can't deal with this.* I opened my heart. *Father, here is my mat of fear. I give it to you. It is yours. I stand against it. I come home where I am safe and I am loved.*

In the midst of my prayers, the worship team sang, "No Longer Slaves." No longer a slave to fear. I am a child of God. I met him in my safest place, my worship.

The song came to an end as I wiped away the remainder of my tears. My hands were visibly shaking.

*Wow, Lord! What have you done?*

Discreetly, I turned to my cousin. "Look."

Held out my hands so she could see how they shook. Tremors had seized my nervous system.

Dee looked at them, then me, then back. "What's wrong?"

"They don't do this unless Jacob's here and I've had an attack. He's not here so I'm thinking God has done something."

We looked at each other, grinned and I whispered, "I'll tell you later what I prayed."

So I walked out of that church unclear on what God did but I SAW and BELIEVED he did something. I had experienced him in many ways in my life, and I knew we could feel and hear him in ways we did not expect.

But I had never felt God use the very thing that had control over me, fear, during worship. He took the "shaking hands" symbol of my fear and showed me how his presence can cause me to tremble.

*Father, that's the kind of shaking hands I CAN live with!*

One week later at 8:30 a.m., I found out exactly what God did that evening at church. I sat in my daughter's counseling session with a grin that would not leave my face.

## TO FORGIVE OR NOT TO FORGIVE

From air that flickered of betrayal, I took a deep breath. Olivia had her first of three court-agreed-upon meetings with her father. We had arrived forty-five minutes early for her prepping session with the therapist.

My child was on edge with high levels of stress. She had expressed to all parties involved she was not ready to see him. My heart, once again, ached. However, we knew we kept everything covered in prayer. We had to trust.

"Three sessions," I told her. "Baby, you can do this."

We went in the office but found no receptionists. So I used the lobby phone.

"Leah, its Laney. We're here."

"Okay. I'll be right out."

After we talked about the agenda, she took Olivia to her office.

Since I had a class as soon as the session was over, I brought extra work to do

Once I sat down in my normal spot, in the corner of the room with my hands empty, I turned on their radio to KLUV, a Christian station. Normally it was on, but with no office staff on Saturdays, I did it. Music to ease the work load and take the edge off the silence.

In the corner I sat with coffee, music, and my cell phone. For the moment I relaxed. Looked through pictures on my phone, deleted some text, sang some songs. I lost track of time and looked up as I heard the door open. Jacob walked in.

Our eyes met. In the seconds it took me to bring my attention back to the phone, I felt a slight flutter-flutter-flutter of my heart. Then it was gone. GONE.

As he walked over to the phone to call Leah—super sensitive to everything my body was not doing—I heard his voice: trigger. We were alone: trigger. Then he sat directly opposite of me. Now I had no way out but past him: huge trigger.

Nothing. While I tried to comprehend what just happened, Millie texted me from her house. I texted back but was so absorbed in this moment: not having to control my breathing, no racing heart, no shaking hands. The flutter had not returned.

Texts went back and forth, but I could not stop smiling. I was not panicking.

*Lord, did you...did you heal me?*

Jacob was messing with his phone. Nothing. I still felt nothing. Kept grinning. This stuck, silly grin on my face.

*You know, Laney, if he looks up and sees you grinning like that while you are on your phone, he is going to think you're talking about him and get really mad.*

Still texting my child, I sent one to Aunt Mamie. Filled her in.

I could not stop my smile.

God had done it. I was healed! I was FREE! I HAD to smile! What JOY I felt!

Sat in the corner of that room without a thought, my insides about to burst with joy.

My aunt had read my text that we were alone, "Remember your bracelet. Rub your bracelet."

"I'm good," I typed.

"Okay...."

"I think I'm healed." Began to text her bits and pieces of what happened at church, along with what he was doing right then and how my body was not responding.

Jacob stood up, walked out and came back in with a drink. Sat back down, played on his phone, stood up again and read the bulletin board. All the while, I hummed along with the radio and did things on my phone. I had given up on the crazy smile leaving my face.

Filled with such raw emotion, I thought I might explode. Though he walked in 15 minutes before, it felt like an eternity. No more doubts. I had been healed, and I was about to cry rivers of tears.

Leah came out to get Jacob. I looked at the time: 8:25. Before I heard the door shut behind them, tears streamed down my face. "Jesus, you healed me! My fear is gone!"

I called Aunt Mamie, and I bawled. Such a sweet release. Together, we celebrated.

My precious, little girl was not celebrating when she came out of that session with her father. But I believed each chain was broken in my daughters and future generations.

After seeing her dad, face to face, for the first time in over two years, Olivia would spend some time with my cousins instead of left alone to deal with the emotional aftermath. Olivia had experienced the effects of the PTSD diagnosis. Now she would experience the result of God's healing. As she celebrated for me while crying through her own tears of anger, I believed one day she would have her own victory.

✝✝✝

I looked back at that morning and was amazed. God had orchestrated every detail to leave not one doubt in my mind. I was healed. His plan was played out in perfect beauty.

When I met with Katelyn, my therapist, I told her everything. We looked at the scenario and laid it out. How I walked into the waiting room and put myself into a corner. He used to back me into corners or places where I had no way out. I trapped myself, unknowingly blocked my own escape route.

We sat in absolute aloneness. Olivia and Leah were behind a keypad-entry locked door. I had met his eyes, heard his voice and he sat right across from me. No way out of this highly-triggered PTSD situation but straight past him.

Katelyn confirmed the perfect scenario for the PTSD to go into a full-blown attack. We could only be amazed together. A professional agreed to what I had known as truth. All the glory went to God.

At the end of our session, she reminded me little moments might happen because of certain triggers or memories.

"That won't mean you're not healed." Katelyn smiled. "Use what you have learned."

"You better believe it won't." Smiled back with a nod in return. "And those moments, I will handle with the word of God."

Within the next two weeks, I saw Jacob at two more sessions. Absolute nothingness. The little flutter in my heart at the first session? That was the Lord as he said, "Feel that, my daughter? Now it's gone."

Eighty-eight days after I had been diagnosed, I was freed. No longer a slave to fear. With hands that no longer shook in fear but trembled from the presence of the Almighty God. Yes!

✝✝✝

On stage one night we sang. Our choir with the worship team, I sang for the first time Free. Amazed at that feeling of Freedom. Free of my fear.

Right there in front of the technology booth, I saw Jacob. He talked to someone, while we practiced. It meant nothing to me. No heart that raced or increased breath or a world around me that started to fade. Nothing. Because that is what freedom was. That is what healed looked like.

So I sang. We were practicing for our Night of Worship: a special night. My excitement stirred.

Rehearsal finished, we waited in the back room. My anticipation built for the service to start. When we lined up, I was delighted to see a full house. This night was purposed to be nothing but praise and worship. As the music began, I experienced the atmosphere in a new way.

How honored I was and what joy to be a part of that service. A year before, I could never have sung as full or as confidently. More of what God's healing felt like. Never had I stood on this stage without fear. Free of PTSD.

God's love—I have only begun to comprehend it.

All those years of abuse gave Millie reasons for hidden emotions, made to feel unworthy to love and never good enough. Those years now affected her future in huge ways. Fear tried to consume her next steps in life, to walk her into that pit of darkness she felt she deserved to be in.

On one hand Millie had taken a big step and exposed herself to tell me how afraid she was of this summer. What would she do after graduation? She opened a place we could talk about it. Shed some light on her fears.

On the other hand, what would she do about this challenge? The opposite of fear is faith and hope. Was there something she hoped for right now, enough to overcome this fear of the future? So she could push through and graduate?

Push through the years of lies, deceit and things that never should have happened to her but did anyway? It angered me. Once more, I fought not to hate him.

Grief filled that place of "What would we be like if...." I felt the loss and mourned in that emptiness. Recurring sadness because of those years of stolen life. It was taken from us. But my mind could not stay in that place of sorrow and resentment.

God is a restorer of ALL things. What was stolen from us, he would return. I had to believe. When would I let go of the loss? Give it up completely so God could do what he was more than exceedingly, abundantly capable of doing in our lives.

Could that release not only change our future but also open us up to absolute forgiveness? Forgiveness that seemed so tricky? Sometimes I thought I had forgiven, then I was at that spot again. To relive the hurt, the hate, and the wounds. All busted apart. Not healed like I thought. Stitched up maybe or covered with a bandage. No, not healed.

For others, forgiveness seemed to happen in an instant. Never to be revisited again. I did not have an answer. I knew true forgiveness was for me, not for Jacob. For the girls, not for their father.

Forgiveness sets us free. With that freedom comes our restoration, God's desire for us.

We did not deserve what happened. It happened anyway. We do not deserve what God has for us. It could happen anyway. But this time it would come from hands that loved us, and promised to protect us, never leave or harm us.

What a hard thing forgiveness can be. But what a precious love this was!

‡‡‡

As I exited the post office that afternoon, my tears left a stain on my cheeks that would be permanent.

The young man, a college student, stood behind me in the most extreme of long lines.

One postal worker at the desk and one at the outside lobby attending the machine. Talk among the customers as we stood in the time-consuming line.

"If you have cash and only need to mail something, you can step out here to the machine," stated the post office lady. "I can help you."

An irate mother in front of me had left the line. A few profane words, dragging her "We are so done with this place" kids along.

"Is the letter all you have?" I asked the student.

"Yes, it's for my admin office but I don't have any cash," he said. "I only have my bank card."

Did I have any cash? I looked in my purse. "Here take this. It should be enough for you to send it."

The young man argued for a second, but I insisted. I knew it would not be more than a buck. He accepted, thanked me and left the line.

An older man now stood beside me. We chatted.

"That was a very gracious thing for you to do."

"Thank you. How kind of you to say that."

I did not know how to accept those words. Almost fell to pieces as I stood there in the post office. Gracious? Had I ever been told something I had done was gracious? Over such a simple thing?

When I made it to my car, sweet tears released and I embraced them. Would I ever forget the elderly gentleman in the post office? Never.

✢✢✢

*Pray for Jacob.*

"Okay, Lord, you know I have already, but I will again. Right now."

So I prayed.

*PRAY for him.*

Pain hit. God saw my heart. He saw the half-hearted way I prayed. I knew I had a choice to make—be obedient or not.

Obedience hurt. As I poured out a prayer, tears flooded the words. Words solely about him, tears meant, by design, for me.

Days later, I felt change inside me. God showed me the scripture in Matthew about the old wine skin and how a new wine cannot be poured into an old wine skin. The old skin cannot hold new wine without bursting.

My tears held the past issues, hurts, abuses I faced. Now given to God to help "dissolve" the old wine skin. My new wine skin was forming.

I felt a new me. God creating a new person inside me. Though I had a long way to go, this was hope: to feel it and live it. Him working in me.

My choices creating our change. Closer to full forgiveness.

✝✝✝

Oh how I cried. I cried for damaged children. For the pain, hurt and scars abuse created. Cried for my child, my sweet daughter. At the hands of her father, she had so many wounds and deep, deep scars. I felt I was running out of time.

Time to be the mother I should have been. To have that mother-daughter relationship I so longed for while she was still in our home. Few precious moments when I pushed through a brick in her wall. Or hugged my child. When I heard her true thoughts or a feeling of what was going on inside her—a rare occurrence.

Those times were worth more than any material thing I owned. Coming up on two years he was out of our house. If her plans went like she wanted, she would leave soon. I cried because I felt I had not become the mother that should have fixed all these damaged, broken pieces. They wedged so tightly between us.

Only God could heal everything broken and fix all the wrongs. While I prayed and waited, I cried. Released tears held back too long that carried with them so much baggage: regret, sorrow, pain, grief, yearning, loss.

Cried because I hoped for a somewhat healed and better, happy, relationship with my child before she moved out. Yet she had pushed me so far away. Brokenness was in my tears.

↓↓↓

It was hard not to hate him. Shaken, I left the office after a session with Leah. Most of the conversation spent on Millie, I had been pierced with an emotional dagger or two. Thrown by the hand of my old enemy—shame.

It had taken me five months after Jacob was out of the home, Thanksgiving Day to be exact, to get past my fear. If Millie told her counselor her dad abused her, would they take my girls from me?

But I saw that Millie could not begin to heal. I still forced her to live under our secrets, our lies. I could not do that anymore because of my own fears. I had to trust a God that had brought us this far. He had been faithful to each word he gave me.

*Why are you afraid?* God asked.

I would obey. I told my daughter to tell her therapist the truth. I promised her we would be okay. I trusted God. Millie trusted me. She told Leah.

I sat in my car and tried to pull myself together before I headed home. I did hate him. I felt intense hate for him. Hate because, in Leah's words, "Damaging her for so long, beginning at such an early age." And "Making her feel like she had to need someone." Now she struggled to find any self worth and could not be alone.

So many reasons to hate him all over again. Tears drowned my face. I ached for her, my baby girl. Felt twinges of guilt and shame I had not felt in a long time.

"Pray harder. She's at a crossroads."

Those were the words Millie's therapist left me with. I dried my eyes, got my emotions under control and prayed. For forgiveness, for help to forgive him, and for my girls. Prayed hard for my girls. Then I gave my precious daughters to the Lord. And drove home to them.

✝✝✝

Pastor started a new series titled No Place like Home. Home meaning God's church. He used comparisons between the church home and our personal homes: our families, inside the home. It hit hard on several aspects in regard to what a home should look like.

While I was busy digesting and working through what I heard, I overlooked the impact it might have had on my daughter.

Her cousin was not there that night, so she had no choice but to listen closer. No preteen distractions. As we followed my family to supper after church, Olivia hit me with a statement that caught my full attention.

"Okay, Mom, it's about to get deep in here."

*This must be serious.* "What's up?" I remained calm.

"So-o-o, you know when pastor was talking about what a home was supposed to be like?"

"Yes."

"Well," Olivia continued, "when Jacob was in the house everyone always had to agree with him. And if we didn't we were wrong. And I never felt…what was that word pastor used?"

"Accepted?"

"Yes. Accepted. I never felt accepted when Jacob was in the house. He never let Millie and me work out our differences. He made us feel they were wrong. And we could never rest. We could never be calm. Now it feels like home. It feels safe and I feel accepted no matter what."

Floored, I parked at the restaurant and looked at my child. The sermon had touched us both, I seized the moment to speak into my daughter the words of wisdom, healing and forgiveness that I prayed everyday for God to give me.

Olivia called her father "Jacob." Not Dad, not my father. His name to be referenced by her was now "Jacob" and her therapist said that was okay. She had her reasons. We all knew why. If that was how she needed to work through her emotions, well, she could call him Jacob.

What insight she received from that message and how it could be used to help heal her! I believed I broke the generational curse of domestic violence in my family. But most times when chains break, they leave behind wounds that need to be healed.

That is God's role. He mends, heals and puts pieces back together. I was nothing short of amazed at some pieces my youngest picked up that night.

$$\downarrow\downarrow\downarrow$$

Forgiveness. Such a beautiful word. Graceful, elegant, and heroic-sounding. Until we have to try to do it. Then it does not seem so pretty. It turns painful, gut-wrenching and almost ugly.

So much seemed to hang on that one word. Revolved around it. How we acted and reacted was affected by it. It seemed to control so much. Seemed unfair one word could have that much power in a person's life.

If this one thing, this one act, could have that much power, why had I not done everything possible to eliminate unforgiveness from my life? My heart? My soul?

Because sometimes it was not that simple. Sometimes I thought I had reached that point of total forgiveness and something happened.

When a crisis arose with my child who still fought issues from being impacted by our abuser. Or perhaps someone that had nothing to do with the situation but happened to do something to remind me of one second in time. INSTANLY all those hurts, wounds and emotions I thought were long gone, healed and forgotten, crashed down. Hate still hid inside.

How many times might this happen until I reached an ultimate place of forgiveness? When I am expected to forgive not only for the wrongs to me but those done to my most precious gifts, my most treasured ones? Will I ever reach a point of total forgiveness?

I have heard of people that claimed to have instant forgiveness of horrible wrongs against them. People who have had instant healings. I am one of those. God is a God of "instants." Some healings come over time though. Through faith and speaking it. I am one of those having to speak forgiveness. It did not come instant for me.

I pray each day for God's grace to forgive, because no way I could get there on my own. But I know it is possible with God.

Piece upon piece, I remind myself, I forgive for me. I remind myself. He died to set me free. I have to set me free, too.

Piece upon piece, I am placed back together again. Something beautiful, this forgiveness thing.

## LEARNING TO LIVE

Years of a life lived in domestic violence produced chains. Chains that bound me in every area. To have thought it only affected what happened inside our home was an illusion. I had been deceived.

Every time I tried to spread my wings to test this new level of freedom, I was reminded of the chains that snapped. The residue of dirt and scraps of metal still clung to my body.

Each move I made, faith HAD to replace fear. Or the step was made in fear anyway. From my first lunch date with a church lady to entering a room full of writers for that first meeting. I walked. Chains were gone.

With my freedom came healing. As I healed came questions. Some were nasty and hard but others pleasant and sweet to my lips.

*Why was the only man who ever laid a hand on me in anger the one I married? Why did I cover him so long?*

*Why didn't I stand up and protect my children better?* I searched for those answers.

Questions I delighted over were *"Wonder if Olivia wants to watch a movie tonight?"* or *"What do I like to paint?" Trees. I love how they could appear dead but for only a season. Then they sprang back to life.*

When I shared my new-found love of tree painting with Aunt Mamie, her response reminded me of another reason I loved her: humor.

"Of course sometimes they truly are dead, dear." She thought she was hilarious.

We laughed. After all, laughter is medicine for the soul.

As I began to learn who I was for the first time in my life, I started to like this person. I even loved me at times.

↓↓↓

Several years ago when I walked out to my car after work, I saw it. A folded yellow paper tucked under my wiper blade with the words "For You" beside a smiley face.

As I looked around for a suspect but found none, I removed it. Inside my car, I read it.

*"Take some time today and listen to 'I Love You More' by Matthew West.*

*You are loved immensely, no matter what, each moment of every day. Even in your darkest hours. You are valued, respected and appreciated. Thank you for making this world a better place.*

*"Find a place inside where there is joy, and the joy will burn out the pain." Joseph Campbell.*

*Praying for you and hope you find the happiness you deserve." — Guardian Angel*

God knew how badly I needed encouragement that day. He provided. Brought another sign of his love into my life to show me I mattered. I was worthy. To help me fight another day. One of many things God did at the perfect time.

I never found out who left that yellow note. Maybe it WAS my guardian angel.

✝✝✝

"Here's a heart. Pick what art supply you want to use. You're artsy, right?" Katelyn handed me the paper.

My therapist had prepared me for what we might do but I had not visualized it. I stared at the outlined heart on the white paper with the blank lines beside it.

"When I'm in the mood and that might not be now," I half-heartily joked.

I had discussed with her that I could not say the girls' father's name unless I was in a situation where I was forced to use it. In fact, I did not even want to refer to him as "my ex." He was "the girls' father," "their dad." If I HAD to mention him, then I would say his name.

To label Jacob as "my ex-husband" somehow connected him to me and I could not do it. I did not need my therapist to analyze all this. I had it figured out correctly. I needed her to help me get back the power he still had in his name.

"You know what? You're right. I don't think I've heard you say his name but a few times in almost a year."

"I don't unless it's a necessity. It's controlled me. So what can we do about it?"

Katelyn's grand idea was to find my medium of choice, add some colors to the heart then label and number the colors with emotions. Bring my huge heart toward healing.

No, I was not up for the emotional display on paper, but knew I had to start somewhere. I would trust Katelyn.

"Okay, I'll try it. Let's use crayons today."

I took the paper, picked out my color scheme of vile expressions and created. Light and dark brown smeared back and forth in opposite directions. Grey and dark grey jaggedly filled in splotches of the heart. Black zigzags went crazy, crossed over each other from one side to the other. Red finalized it, filling in little spots so tiny they were almost hidden within the other colors.

"Now label each color with the emotion it connects to you."

*Bring this train wreck of a heart some meaning?* As I looked at my artwork, my eyes were opened. It did hold symbolism. I labeled.

- light brown: disgust
- dark brown: sickened
- grey: tense
- red: guarded
- dark grey: connected
- black: revolted

"Okay, I did it."

"Now number them from the strongest emotion you feel when you say his name to the least."

"Wow, this exercise looked so simple."

It was not. I had to think about Jacobs's name. Say it in my head. Experience it to recall emotions that I did not want. Feel them and "judge" them. I was nauseous.

1. Disgust

2. Tense

3. Sickened

4. Revolted

5. Connected

6. Guarded

"This week your homework is to set a timer for five minutes and see how many times you can say his name. Begin with that timeframe and increase it. Do you want to keep your drawing?"

"Katelyn, I will gladly let you hold onto my heart for now." I smiled with a wink.

↓↓↓

It took several days to sit down for that first homework attempt. With the timer set for five minutes, I prayed in anticipation for a rough few minutes of speaking Jacob's name out loud.

With worship music on my laptop, I was soothed. As a song I loved singing for months flooded my senses, something hit me. The artist's first name was the same as HIS. Had I somehow been blinded to that fact? I had not connected it until this second.

Lyrics that encouraged me to hold nothing back but give everything to the Lord. Which was what I needed to do, right now, with Jacob's name. Give the Sick, Disgust, Revolted and all the other emotions that harmed and controlled me in a name TO the name of Jesus.

"Jacob…Jacob…Jacob…."

I sang that song. I worshiped. "God, I give you his name. Jacob. Jacob."

I cried. I felt the ugly and the connection lifted. No longer trapped or ensnared by kindergarten ABC's. After all, it was only a name, right? Made up of letters.

A new level of freedom again. Now, it WAS only a name: Jacob. It could not hurt me anymore.

A couple days later I was back in Katelyn's office, excited to share the news.

"I hope you're prepared with a heart because I can say Jacob's name without an issue. God walked me right through it."

"What happened?" She reached into her folder."You bet I have one!"

We laughed and I set about choosing my colors of deliverance. As I told Katelyn how God freed me, I used crayons to design a quite opposite piece.

This time I chose red, turquoise, blue, purple, magenta, and a blue-green. I started with a circular spot of red in the center of the heart. It was surrounded with the next color and the next. Each one merging, splashing into a heart shape as it blended into the next color.

None numbered, only the emotions labeled.

Red: Prevailed.

Turquoise: Content.

Blue-green: At peace.

Blue: Calm.

Purple: Relieved.

Magenta: Finished.

That was my order. Simplistic, yet simply beautiful.

↓↓↓

Most of my days passed with Jacob as a fleeting memory. Less and less triggers and things to remind me of him. The shame, guilt and anger slowly lifted from my shoulders. A heavy burden removed made a pathway to forgiveness and freedom less rocky.

Never to forget God could heal in an instant. He healed my PTSD. To look and remember how far I had come. Yet give myself the grace God gives me in knowing I am still a process. A process he is working on. Not everything he does in me is instantaneous.

What were those words I spoke to myself in moments like these? When I had to pray for forgiveness, AGAIN, because I felt anger at Jacob, AGAIN. One of our daughters had compared herself to him, and it was not a positive quality she used.

Millie, the daughter who suffered most at his hand, had expressed this comparison to her kid sister. Used it to excuse her own actions and behavior in her current relationship. Blamed the abuse she endured from her father for how she treated her boyfriend. While excusing her father's behavior based on his own abuse in childhood.

"That's why Dad can't control his anger sometimes. Because of stuff he told us that happened to him when he was a kid. That's why I can't control my anger, because of what he's done to me."

Olivia vented. "He can't use his past to make it okay why he hurt all of us, any more than you can use what he did to make how you're acting okay."

As I listened to this twisted conversation played out between my daughters, my heart was devastated. A part of Millie believed she showed abusive tendencies same as her dad to people she was in relationship with. Even excused his behavior.

Yet Olivia was not blinded or deceived. She was not about to let her big sister cop out of accepting responsibility because of their abusive dad. Or toss his behavior aside due his own childhood.

I had seen so much growth in my daughters these past few years. But in conversations like this, I knew there was so much more healing needed. How could one child see so clearly while the other have a vision splotched in darkness?

Jacob. He was in Millie's head as he had been in mine.

*God help me not to hate him. Help me to forgive him. Help me help my daughters to forgive him. Help me to help Millie see the truth.*

✝✝✝

This man had thrown my emotions back to a time when much of my days were spent trying to overcome a state of constant anxiety and fear. A relative of my former husband made another attempt to engage with me. Why?

Jacob had remarried, but I saw no reason why I needed to befriend his family at this time in my life. I would never be rude or hateful to them but they were my abusive ex-husband's family. We had no relationship with him. Why would I encourage one with his family?

After the service, Dee and I were in the lobby, wrapped up in dinner plans with the girls. Sunglasses on my head, I reached for them as we were about to leave.

"Well, I've missed seeing you lately!"

Based on the tone and delight in the voice, I turned around with expectations of it being someone relatively familiar to me. Prepared that he might expect a hug. Hugs that I do not give easily.

I was blindsided by him. My body reacted fast and I switched the sunglasses from one hand to the other: the hugging arm.

"Nice to see you."

I did not smile. No force in my body allowed it to happen.

He turned and trotted away.

My cousin's wife and I stared at each other. Speechless. Immovable.

"What was THAT?" Dee whispered.

"I don't have a clue but let's get out of here please."

It tried to close in around me. The old panic and fear. *Could it be happening again?*

Behind the wheel, alone, I drove to my cousin's home after church. Olivia had ridden home with them. Good thing. I was a mess.

"I see a beautiful sunset. I see my bracelet that tells me all I need is faith the size of a mustard seed. I see my verse 'no weapon formed against me shall prosper,'" I half-spoke, half-cried my 5-5-5's from therapy.

The words rolled off my tongue. Tears streamed down my face as what felt like ages ago, I had to bring myself back from "that place."

Angry, emotional and bawling, I had to get to the heart of why it had affected me this strongly. I WOULD overcome it. He would not have this power over my emotions.

"Father, show me why this man's hug has done this to me."

It was revealed. At that moment, I felt as if I was back to that place when I had the protection order on Jacob and he had reached me through someone else.

As I began to come back to the state of mind I needed to be in, the woman God freed, more words found air. "Satan, you cannot do anything to me God has not allowed. Where you come at me in one way, you must flee in seven."

My eyes glanced down at the tattoo on my wrist that steered the car. With more strength in my voice, "He whom the son sets free is free indeed." My eyes shifted to the other wrist, "I am unashamed and I will praise your name because you are the God who broke all my chains."

When I parked the car in Elliot and Dee's driveway, calmness and control had returned. Not only did I have victory over an attack, I found revelation on why it happened. Was I still healed? Absolutely!

┼┼┼

To have survived something can be a miraculous event. Nothing can compare. It should not be downplayed or minimized. When a person gets to the other side—the "I survived" or "I am a survivor" side—the story is often a miracle.

My own experiences, so many times in my life, I ONLY survived by God's grace and intervention. I call that the working of miracles. Survived many obstacles that were meant to destroy, damage and keep me in despair and darkness.

At times some of these things were meant to kill me. Even though I had forsaken my God, he promised to never forsaken me. I survived. Through him, by him and for him. I would never diminish the act of survival. It is POWERFUL.

But now I need more. I want to eliminate everything domestic violence left me with: pain, side effects, aftermath, stigma. Every single thing that can affect and stifle my future in a negative way. Now I need to overcome. I am not content to stay in survival status.

No longer a survivor, but an overcomer. No longer survive the temptation but overcome the addiction. Not only beat the disease but overcome the stigma it left behind. Or simply survive a past that damaged but overcome the anguish and ugly inside. Let it be replaced with peace and beauty.

I fought within my freedom to remember I am not an addiction, a disease or my past. I am not a temptation, a stigma or ashamed. I am a survivor. I have a choice to be more. I am an OVERCOMER.

↓↓↓

As I knelt down at the patio doors for a close-up of our albino-splotched squirrel, I knew we would miss her with the move. I marveled at the transitions that had happened in my life. One of which would be huge in the future of my girls. Several doors cracked open that could be God opportunities I believed for. These excited me. Other than the prophetic pieces he gave me, I had no clue where they might lead.

I prayed and I trusted. How would God use me, walk with me, to change my daughters' futures, my generation's destiny? How many lives could be changed for his glory as I choose to obey?

Sometimes the sense of running out of time before I accomplish what God has planned overwhelmed me. Past choices tried to haunt me.

I sat in my therapist's office after months of a guilt-free life. A strong stab in my heart and sudden tears trickled down my checks.

Angered at myself, I looked into Jessie's eyes.

In silence, the clinical psychologist waited for me to gather myself. The women's shelter where I received my counseling for over four years had one flaw. Though it was a system that had to operate that way for the therapists and I quite understood it, the retelling of "my story" at the start of "another year, another intern" was my sore spot.

In the midst of connections being made with my artwork, piecing together brokenness with Millie and Olivia maturing into an insightful preteen, I had closed a closet. In it remained what was left of my guilt. I collapsed into a place I thought no longer existed.

Our conversations had been about talk of the future, plans and goals. It turned to tears and terrors.

"Why does it anger you that you're crying, Laney?"

"Because I thought it was a place I was done with. It could not rule my actions, thoughts or BODY any longer. Yet here I am with a tissue."

"So if possible lack of time can be used to make you feel guilt then what could you do about that? Do you believe you should continue to feel shame and guilt?

*Did part of me still feel I was responsible for the abuse to my girls? Had I locked a little piece of guilt up because I owned it? It was my burden and I felt unworthy to let it go.*

This was my chance to swing that door wide open. I knew I could not harbor guilt. It would allow every monster back into my dreams and thoughts that God and I had battled so hard to kick out. I would not let it stay hidden to ambush me again.

"I have to remember that I live in the plans for each day, concern myself with it. God will worry about tomorrow. His timing is perfect. He freed me from the guilt and shame. All those feelings, Jesus carries for me because he loves me that much."

I walked into Jessie's office expecting to chat about good things that had happened. I left my appointment with makeup not so perfect. A little less dust and debris from those broken, rusted old chains now clung to my body. God was good.

"Oh, Father!"

The words fell off my lips and rose into the air ever so slowly due to the weight they carried. He knew my heart. Every thought, every intention, every feeling. I may as well voice it.

"Please don't let her die. For me, Lord. I can't take it!"

The words took wings and flew. No longer heavy.

Released and unburdened of my worst fear for Aunt Mamie, tears of relief fell. The guilt that had hindered those words gone. I knew how many would be devastated by the loss of my aunt, so I laid on my bed withholding true feelings from a God who knew them already. Because I felt selfish.

But why should I feel selfish for loving the woman who held so many facets in my life? Aunt, spiritual mother, best friend, confidant, mentor...so much more.

I did not think I would survive the loss of two dear women in my life so close together.

It had been slightly over a year since my mother had passed from cancer. We had come to share a special bond over dolls and jewelry. The last several years, mom had perfected her skill at sending me the perfect bracelets from Alabama for different occasions. No more talks about a Walgreens visit gone bad or her latest ring purchase gone well. I missed her.

The thought of losing my aunt was incomprehensible. My heart and tears poured out on the pillow. Prayer was everything and all I could do. Aunt Mamie was on a cruise ship in another country, in a foreign hospital. Maybe heartburn. Maybe a heart attack. Maybe they did not know.

"I've surrendered all my fears to you, Lord. You are a miracle God. I will stand strong and trust."

A few days later, one of Aunt Mamie's daughter in laws and I sat in the airport waiting for a plane to land. Uncle Abe had kept our secret. Aunt Mamie, alive and kicking, was in for a surprise greeting. She had suffered a mild heart attack but no permanent damage and had been flown home.

To be in that airport to see my aunt when she came through that gate was my only choice. I had to touch my answered prayer.

✝✝✝

The usual black coffee in hand, I sat in Olivia's therapist's office. Opened my planner to work. I glanced up and stopped. It was there. The first painting in my series I had started over three years ago.

It hung on the wall, revealed to all while still protected within its black frame in the waiting room. The board had agreed to hang it in their lobby and I had eagerly awaited its unveiling. All alone in the room, I giggled like a little girl at the sheer disbelief that it happened.

I stood up and took a picture of my picture in case someone realized it was not so good and took it down. What if they concluded an awful mistake had been made? This time next week, would it be snatched from the spot it now occupied?

Fear rambled, and I recognized it. I would enjoy this moment, this dream for me. To see my print "Hope in the Darkness" on the wall of a place that brings hope to so many touched me deeply.

*God, you have brought us so far. Look at what you have done in our lives.*

With more than thirty minutes left of Olivia's time with Leah, my joy simmered and overflowed. *What had God done?*

Amelia moved here last year so all three of my daughters, with my grandchild, now lived in the same state as me. Millie and I had a better relationship now than we have ever had: open, honest and mending. Olivia continued to find her strength and voice in her own individuality. Relationships and bonds that had never been between all three sisters formed.

Weight loss continued for me. As I found more root causes for the issues, I lost and kept off almost a hundred pounds. I had battled ups and downs with my weight all my life.

I was now secure in saying, "Battle won."

People-pleasing for me was an art form. How could I handle any confrontation or disagreements? Those situations terrified me and I was not equipped.

Yet here I was. Learning how to say "No" when I could not do something asked of me or maybe agreeing at a different time.

I did not have to give an excuse for each time I missed a text or a phone call, why I could not meet for a certain time.

Little revelations, but huge freedom.

A fundraiser I was blessed to be a participant in: a print of another painting of mine sold to benefit people. The experience I gained was irreplaceable. Humility coupled with the sound of rejoicing. I was blessed with lessons I would never had been able to afford.

I marveled at the people God placed in my life, if only for a season, to help me grow. They played such a huge part in how I was stretched, blessed and transformed. When had I begun to build my tiny pieces of trust with such HUGE trust issues?

"It was all you wasn't it, Jesus?"

*When I thought I could not trust another word out of another person's mouth, you showed me it was possible.*

The master puzzle maker started putting pieces of "me" back together: tiny piece of Trust fit, huge piece of Fear did not, that smooth piece called Self-Worth connected. Another one named Shame too jagged to mesh tossed aside but the one called Loved found its perfect place.

Not only had I started to feel more confident on the inside, courage built up to try a new hairstyle for my outer self. In the words of my new hairstylists it would be "less traditional." So for my 50<sup>th</sup> birthday, I did it. A hairstyle that was modern and shorter than I ever had yet still me. I LOVED it.

Lost in all those thoughts of goodness, time with the therapist sped by. Leah and Olivia chattered as my daughter opened her "reward" bag of goldfish.

"You guys hung up my picture."

Leah laughed, "We did. It took a little longer because of a few office things. It was actually up last time you were in."

"You're kidding me! How did I miss it? That's crazy!" I smiled as I grabbed my phone.

"Can we get a picture with it?"

As Olivia turned into our professional photographer, I wrapped my arm around the girls' therapist I had come to love and respect. We smiled for the camera. Another defining moment to add to my new life.

↓↓↓

"Look Ma, I bought this for you," Millie's voice full of excitement.

"What is it?" Olivia piped in.

My middle child had walked in from work at the clothing store. With her generous heart and latest finds, she reached into the big shopping bag.

"I cannot imagine what it is but let's see, Hon."

Out came this beautiful dress. Graphic black and white print on the top with a draped neckline and sleek, solid black skirt.

"So Ma, I took an hour trying on different dresses until I found one I thought would look great on you. Do you like it?"

"Wow! That was a lot of time and effort for me. I think it's beautiful. Thank you!"

"You know, it has been over two years since Dad's been gone so I think it's time you started dating. Now you have a dress that fits since you've lost so much weight," Millie declared, quite pleased with herself.

"That's what you think, huh? What about you, Olivia?" I teased.

When my daughters' opinions bubbled out, I listened as they burst into chatter and openness. I reveled at another piece of freedom. This dress had shown me how far my girls had come. They felt safe to share their thoughts. They were in relationship with each other. It did not always have to be perfect but it was a relationship, and they were discussing my happiness.

*God! We must be on the right track. Thank you, Father, for these girls.*

With much delight at what the "date dress" had actually become to me, I thanked my sweet daughter for the gift with a promise of "I'll think about a date when I'm ready."

What I felt that day is even stronger almost three years later. Almost five years since Jacob has been gone. I have yet to wear that date dress. Not one date. I do not date. I believe to date is to be looking for a mate. My priorities have been to learn for the first time in my life who I was without all these things:

- No sexual, physical, emotional or psychological abuse
- No drugs, alcohol or cigarettes that I was freed from over eighteen years ago
- Fight the food fight and win

What food DO I like? I play around with the simple things such as brands of coffee: dark, bold, rich and black equals perfect. Even my favorite lifetime color of purple took second as a new one, red, emerged.

To lose the victim mentality, believe who I am in Christ and how much he truly loves me and wants me safe. To grow into the mother, grandmother, worshiper, writer and artist God says I am. To grow closer and closer to the One who set me free and continues to each day.

I am content. Do I get lonely once in awhile? Sure. But I am content. I am learning to love me, with a love as my Father loves me. No more joy trickles. Now I have joy tsunamis.

So one day if a man shows up holding that sign or slips me a note that reads "This is what the Lord told me to tell you..." and it matches what I was told, then I know I have my husband. My little joke to those who ask.

†††

If only I had not stayed almost nineteen years. What if my daughters had never had to endure all the pain, abuse, heartache and loss? Could I have prayed harder for Jacob? Why didn't Jacob change? Why didn't he just CHANGE?

These questions and thoughts used to torment me. Used to shame and guilt me until I thought I might go insane. Still I must hold it together on the outside. After all I had kept it locked up tight all my life, what was any different now?

But I knew. Now I had nothing to numb all the pain. I felt every stab, prick, heard every whisper and "what if," saw every video play again and again in my head. I hurt so bad, I could not take it anymore. How could I have been so blinded to allow my most precious possessions to exist in a life of abuse day after day?

After taking care of some business with my attorney, we talked pleasantries. I considered Sheena my friend.

"How are you doing?"

"I'm fine."

"Okay, Laney. We all know what fine means. You're not."

After I unloaded most of the truth and saved the worst for Jesus, I waited. Weak. I had always tried to stay strong. Even with my therapists and especially with Sheena.

"It's okay to scream you know."

We were at a quiet stare down. Her attorney "I can see right through this" smile and my "I don't know what you're talking about" look.

"No I can't." My defenses broke.

"Why not?"

"Because if I scream and all this stuff I feel inside me comes out, I might not find my way back."

"I promise you…you will make it back. You will still be strong. Go to a park or your basement or somewhere no one can hear you and scream, cry or whatever you need to do. Let all these feeling and emotions out. Release them. They're hurting you."

Tears and tissues ended the meeting that day. Another Godsend in this adventure. The attorney who fought to protect my daughters and me, kept us safe. The attorney who still held a special place in my heart.

☩☩☩

No longer do I play the game of Q&A. No longer will I live under shame and guilt. Those things kept me in my past. These things are not my burdens to carry. They belong to the Lord. He is my strength. He is why I will still be strong.

A future is what I want for my children, grandchildren and me. One that is free from emotional, physical, sexual and psychological abuse. A future free of addictions and chains that bind and torture.

God will heal us from our past. Restore what was taken. Mend everything back together. He has more for us than what we thought we lost. He has forgiven me and I had to forgive myself. As I forgive others, I heal.

No longer do I need to wear my treasure I found in the bookstore that day. But I will forever stand upon the reminder "All things are Possible" that dangled from the bracelet. Elegant font engraved into the sterling silver around the encased mustard seed. The perfect representation of the Word of God.

Now it gleams from my car mirror. Faith of a mustard seed. To remind me to always have faith.

To take that step in trust, the one step that sets me FREE!

# ACKNOWLEDGEMENTS

To my most precious treasures: my three daughters. Amanda, Megan and Maddie. You girls put your trust in me when trust was something I struggled to hold onto in others. You called me strong. I call you girls the strong ones.

Bev: Without your wisdom, guidance and unconditional love for me, I might have crumbled under the weight of this life.

Auntie Tammy: The many late night phone calls because we knew there was no one else awake but us, right when we needed each other—priceless. What would I do without you?

My mother: Though you will never read this as you are with the Lord in Heaven, I thank you for teaching me strength. Because now I see, you had to be a strong woman. I miss you, Mother.

Devin and Heather: You both filled a place in my heart that was so empty and lost. All the things you guys did that made my girls and me feel cared for and special will never be forgotten.

Tyson and Quincy: My cousins, including Devin, you are more my brothers than my cousins. Some of the best men I know with the biggest hearts.

Heather T.: Thank you for your faithfulness. Never have I doubted that if prayer was needed, you would pray. You are valued in so many ways! I love you.

Gary: My favorite comedian. Uncle, you can make me laugh at times when it's not even appropriate. One of the many reasons I love you.

My siblings: Thank you for being a part of my life. I love you all dearly. Thanks for the support you have given me through this whole adventure. You guys are GREAT!

My Pastors: Thank you for being the real thing, living what you preach. Creating a desire, in me, for the Lord that is unquenchable.

Debora B: Thank you for pouring your time and talent into me. Speaking into me words of inspiration and truth. You have been my confidence-builder and my friend.

Rhonda M: You have pushed me out of my box so many times. How we were beautifully woven together! Thank you for being a special part of my world.

Jenny R: My "above and beyond" neurologist. You spoke into me when it was not in your job description. You are a Blessing to my life. You are loved.

My Choir Family: I walked into that green room frightened and intimidated without one person I knew, besides the choir director. But you welcomed me and all my flaws. I now have a family.

Laura C: Thank you for the talks and good times. We have had a wonderful choir experience together. The coffees we have shared could buy a Starbucks!

SafeHome: To the Counselors who walked me through the pain of domestic violence. Each one of you were exactly who I needed at that exact time.

Susanna C: For serving, protecting and being the best attorney I could have ever dreamed for my girls and me. Always counseling and representing me with integrity and respect. Thank you for being a woman I am now honored to call my friend.

Lifelines: To the counselor who invested into the lives of my girls. Thank you for the part you have played in their road to healing.

RJT: My writing coach! Our paths were beautifully lined up from day one. You have been one of my biggest fans and encouragers. I cannot wait to see where we go from here!

My Prayer Team: You Mighty Women of Valor prayed me through times you know about and others only God knows. I will never be able to thank you enough.

To every person who has supported this cause in any way, I thank you so very much! I could not possibly name you all. I could not have written this book without the prayers, shares, follows, financial help and support.

I thank these talented men Aaron D. and Greg M., for my headshots.

My Dad, other Aunts, Uncles, cousins, nieces, friends that have so impacted our lives. I am honored to be a part of yours.

Above all, to my First Love: Thank you. You waited on me to find my way home. I am home.

# ABOUT THE AUTHOR

Laney Wind is an Autism Paraprofessional in the Kansas City, Kansas area. She has earned college credits in an Interpreter Training Program for Sign Language for the Deaf.

She has three daughters and the youngest often gets accused of being spoilt by the other two siblings. Laney has the luxury of all her children living close by and the joys of experiencing her first grandchild who happens to be a boy with possibly the best sense of humor one would ever come across in a four year old. A joy!

Besides a love for family, Laney has found a love for writing. It began in childhood with preteen poems written to express silliness and beauty, then hurt and pain. Intertwined with the love for writing Laney discovered sketching and painting.

But beauty can come from ashes. During the past five years, Laney has embraced and developed her heart for music, writing and art. To find freedom in expressing worship in each one. And learning to live in the peace in which the Maker of these gifts brings.

Each day is a step forward. Each day an opportunity.

Each Day Matters.

Made in the USA
Columbia, SC
01 March 2020

88556526R00137